I AM WHO I AM
NATIVE BLACK AMERICAN
NOT AFRICAN AMERICAN

I AM WHO I AM

NATIVE BLACK AMERICAN

NOT AFRICAN AMERICAN

MILTON B. HAZZARD

CITI OF BOOKS

CITIOFBOOKS, INC.
3736 Eubank NE Suite A1
Albuquerque, NM 87111-3579
www.citiofbooks.com
Hotline: 1 (877) 389-2759
Fax: 1 (505) 930-7244

Ordering Information:
Quantity sales. Special discounts are available on quantity purchases by corporations, associations, and others. For details, contact the publisher at the address above.

Printed in the United States of America.
ISBN-13:   Paperback   979-8-89391-605-8
             eBook   979-8-89391-607-2
             Hardback   979-8-89391-606-5

Library of Congress Control Number: 2025905559

"WE UNDERSTAND... WE DO NOT, WE CAN'T OVERLOOK THE CONNECTION TO AFRICA. BUT... WE ARE WHO WE ARE. NATIVE BLACK AMERICANS."

Hazzard delves into the intricate question of what the term "African American" truly signifies, providing his own insightful answer. He ultimately arrives at the thought-provoking realization that this label fails to accurately encompass the identity of Black individuals born on American soil. Instead, he advocates for the designation of "Native Black Americans," emphasizing that these individuals are not just part of the fabric of the nation but are its natural-born citizens. Throughout this enlightening journey, the author skillfully navigates the rich tapestry of history, exploring the vast array of terms that have been employed over time to identify the Black population born in America. Each label, he notes, tells a different story, reflecting the cultural, social, and political shifts that have shaped their identities.

In his work, Hazzard employs quotations from the Bible to substantiate his arguments, alongside historical events that facilitate readers' comprehension of his perspective regarding the appropriate designation for black individuals born in the United States as Native Black Americans. The author explores the larger issue of labeling and the tendency of individuals to categorize those they perceive as different. Hazzard recognizes that some readers may identify with experiences of being inaccurately labeled based on their appearance. For example, he asserts that black individuals born on American soil should be designated as Native Black Americans, as referring to them as African Americans can lead to misconceptions. Furthermore, the author addresses the challenge of external labeling that fails to represent these individuals accurately, often stemming from bigotry or prejudice. Readers interested in studies on ethnicity or who are frustrated by inadequate racial labels may find themselves intrigued by the author's unique viewpoint.

-**The US Review of Books**
Profession Reviews for the People
Reviewed by Amanda Hanson

Table of Contents

INTRODUCTION

Abraham Lincoln, President of the United States of America issued two (2) Emancipation Proclamations. The first announcement was dated September 22, 1862. It was approved according to the provisions of The Second Confiscation Act and The Militia Act. The document had words to this effect. The slaves in all areas designated as being in rebellion as of January 1,1863, would "be then, thenceforward, and forever free."

When the States in rebellion did not give approving answers, President Lincoln placed the second Emancipation Proclamation into effect.

We are reminded that when using the Bible as a reference, the number eight (8) talks to a new creation...a new beginning. A new creation for the purposes of this writing talks about a new racial name. Exodus 3:14 KJV reminds us "I Am That I Am." Accepting that as a truth and using it as a motivation source. Let it be known...**I am "A NATIVE BLACK AMERICAN."**

African American is a misused, racially centered title often powered through self-appointed supremacy. It is also used by people seeking to be politically correct. Accepting African American...suggests that some Black people are willing to sacrifice self-respect while trying to find a racial identity that is not blemished. African American is blemished because it is an open-ended name covering people from many Countries. Users focus on assumed shared African and Native Black American similarities. However, the main differences between the two are often ignored. At the end of the day, using African American does not represent a choice held by all Black People who were born in the United States of American soil, dust, or clay.

Rise early, early in the morning. Look upwards towards the East. Watch and pray while God presides over the rising sun to create one more day. Another creation is also revealed. It is without blemish, it is dignified, and a true racial identity. Native Black American. How great are His works.

CHAPTER ONE
The Summer Chapter

"Let the words of my mouth, and the meditation of my heart, be acceptable in thy sight, O Lord, my strength, and my redeemer." Psalm 19:14 KJV.

Lift your eyes towards the Eastern skyline as the sun rises. Genesis 1:1 KJV reveals "In the beginning God created the heaven and the earth."

The Bible does not specifically identify a year when the earth and universe were created. Therefore, we submit and accept that other than the time given "in the beginning" no one knows the specifics surrounding the beginning of time. The truth is…it really does not matter…it did happen.

As a stand-alone. The statement "in the beginning" may cause a lot of inquiring minds to suppose that the scripture referred to is too difficult. The truth is, some doubt several Biblical stories. They want touchable logic.

Human nature nourishes such behavior. For some the creation question can linger as a mystery, but their quality of positive faith is not affected.

Nevertheless, just speaking the words "in the beginning" strongly puts forward evidence that a first step was taken in a series of actions or steps taken to achieve a pre-determined goal…creation.

Admittedly from time to time "just believing" can be a challenge, but it is wise to accept the mysteries of God with a discipline that pushes away questions or doubts. Proverbs 3:5 KJV tells us "Trust in the Lord with all thine heart; and lean not unto thine own understanding."

Most writers of various versions of the Bible seem to keep away from the actual age of the earth and universe. Scholars and scientists point out that the earth and universe could be billions of years old. Sometimes they try to determine Earth's age by examining the scriptures and other written or spoken references. Sometimes they rely on a scientific discipline called carbon dating.

Carbon dating is using science-based logic and principles to estimate the age of things that began existence as a living matter.

Isaiah 40:28 KJV gives this counsel. "Hast thou not known? hast thou not heard, that the everlasting God, the Lord, the Creator of the ends of the earth, fainteth not, neither is weary? there is no searching of his understanding."

We do not believe…that God is looking over His shoulder!

With a focus on biblical philosophy the number 4 is associated with intentional design or appointed times.

Intentional design or appointed times can be associated with Genesis 1:14 KJV which tells us, "And God said, Let there be lights in the firmament of the heaven to divide the day from the night; and let them be for signs, and for **seasons**, and for days, and years."

The word seasons can point to intentional dividing. 4 different seasons are divided and named. 4 different seasons have 4 different climatic conditions.

In general, much of the planet that we call the earth experiences four seasons in a year. Those seasons change by the circling of the earth around the sun caused by the strong gravity pull from the sun. Keep in mind that the exposure of the earth to heat from the sun will increase or decrease as the earth tilts to the right or left while it circles the sun.

The four climatic seasons include.
1. Summer.
2. Fall.
3. Winter.
4. Spring.

In this writing you will find use of the word season to identify each chapter.

Think of a proposal to adjust one racial classification. To be Specific, we strongly suggest replacing the racial title African American which is often incorrectly assigned to Black citizens born in the United States.

African American is a title which is open to many different opinions, judgements, and different meanings to different people. It provokes a most confusing National racial identification. We do have in mind the creation of a new beginning. One that is unblemished. *Native Black American.*

How can it be that Black people born in the United States are the only race on earth that has been subjected to 7 different racial names? For a divine reason? From a religious standpoint 7 stirs up perfection and completion.

Let us consider this. A White person of European origin born on the soil of Africa and has African citizenship, then migrates to the United States. With the passing of time the same person is given U.S. citizenship. Are they African Americans?

Let us consider this. A person of Asian origin born on the soil of Africa and has African citizenship, then migrates to the United States. With the passing of time the same person is given U.S. citizenship. Are they African Americans?

Let us consider this. A person of Hispanic or Latino origin born on the soil of Africa and has African citizenship, then migrates to the United States. With the passing of time the same person is granted U.S. citizenship. Are they African Americans?

Let us consider this. A person of the Pacific Islands origin born on the soil of Africa and has African citizenship, then migrates to the United States. With the passing of time the same person is given U.S. citizenship. Are they African Americans?

Let us consider any person of any race, with any skin color, born on the soil of Africa and has African citizenship, then migrates to the

United States. With the passing of time the same person is given U.S. citizenship. Are all immigrants from Africa of any race… identified as African Americans?

Once again…we submit that the word African American is open to countless different opinions and understandings. Quite honestly. It seems to be an attempt to deny Native Black Americans of their constitutional privileges earned by birth entitlement. Native Black Americans are not refugees, immigrants, or a people with a thirst to kidnap someone else's racial identity. God said "I Am That I Am." We say…we are who we are.

Contrary to an opinion supposedly held by many…African American is not a name preferred by the majority of those it allegedly describes. Black people born in the United States. I ask anyone willing to hear. By what authority did the racial title African American gain the status of being marketed as our official racial designation? Hearing that, any justification given is cast adrift as a fake.

Please understand that this is not just an interest held exclusively by this author. There is a silent majority who agree with many of the opinions expressed in this writing.

Often, we like to blame events, but we choose a path to walk through life. Our decisions will lead to either a good or a bad outcome.

In the past we may not have applied very much effort to influence the path of our race naming. Here and now without hesitation, we must seize this opportunity and take part in this new creation, Native Black American.

For unknown reasons. When the Bible was being written, you will notice that there are 400 years of word silence between the Old Testament and New Testament. History tells us that in the year 1619, a number of African captives were unloaded onto the shores of Jamestown. Those humans were sold into slavery. This writing was conceived during the year 2019, 400 years after 1619. Could the number 400 suggest a spiritually inspired time and season for this new beginning? Adoption of a new racial name.

Carefully chosen holy wordings were judged to be proper for inclusion in bible which is the oldest continually published book in accepted history.

Please note that this writing relies in part on viewpoints found in The King James Version of the Holy Bible (KJV). (Publisher: Public Domain).

King James I, who also held the title King James VI, was James Charles Stuart. He is accredited with being involved in bringing together the King James version of the bible (KJV). We could not find with unquestionable accuracy the total time spent finishing the translations. Research did reveal that the process of translating words or text from selected sources into the KJV bible was achieved by a committee of scholars and clergymen.

The KJV of the Bible, commissioned in 1604 and first published in 1611 does have certain adjustment to language usage and reasoning that may reflect differently when compared to other versions of the Bible.

Please understand that many ideas and truths quoted in this writing reflect opinions expressed by writers of the KJV. Our objective was to call on established knowledge as a source of wisdom.

This effort of this writing is to point out that racial labelling used to quench a thirst for discrimination is not ok simply because "that's just the way it has always been." We challenge for change. We challenge humanity to follow the wisdom and examples given from God through the scriptures.

The United States of America is a very successful Country. Our objective is to contribute to helping the United States of America be a better Country.

We will reflect on the importance of fishing from the right side of the ship or doing the right thing according to the will of God. As we march into the opinions discussed in this writing, we are reminded of wisdom referenced in John 15:5 KJV. "For without me ye can do nothing."

That statement sends this strong message. Those who attempt to bring about change relying solely on personal power without seeking the blessing of God may appear to succeed for a while.

But…without the blessing of God the effort will in the long, run find limited if any success. On the other hand, if one chooses to fish from the right side of the ship there is hope. Matthew 19:26 KJV "with God all things are possible."

Genesis 2:2 KJV tells us "And on the seventh day God ended his work which he had made; and he rested." Genesis 2:7 KJV tells us "And the Lord God formed man of the dust of the ground." Inquiring minds will have to accept that the creation day and location is one of God's mysteries.

Perhaps when focusing on the words "God formed man of the dust" it may be helpful to associate the word dust with another word… clay.

Our inspiration for that suggestion is found in Isaiah 64:8 KJV. "But now, O Lord, thou art our father; we are the clay, and thou our potter; and we all are the work of thy hand."

Think about this. When He created man, God had the power to use any valuable substance of his choice. But he chose dust, or said another way, clay. Just another miracle performed by God, where is your faith?

We believe that when the Bible describes the forming of man from dust the intent was to highlight God's supernatural power and His humbleness. Could it be that the intent of God was to instill humbleness in his people?

Isaiah 55:8-9 KJV tells us: "For my thoughts are not your thoughts, neither are your ways my ways, saith the Lord. For as the heavens are higher than the earth, so are my ways higher than your ways, and my thoughts than your thoughts."

As we continue in Genesis 1:10 KJV. "And God called the dry land Earth; and the gathering together of the waters called he called Seas."

The Bible tells us in Genesis 2:8 KJV "And the Lord God planted a garden eastward in Eden; and **there he put** the man whom he had formed." Of interest…He did not say it was the first man that He had created.

As previously stated, the number 8 talks to a new beginning. Do you believe it a coincidence that God inspired a reference to his creation or a new beginning in a scripture that included the number 8? Genesis 2:8.

There were 4 rivers associated with the location of the Garden of Eden. However, the exact location of the Garden can be a matter of debate.

Genesis 2:8 KJV "And the Lord God planted a garden eastward in Eden; and there he put the man whom he had formed."

But watch this. Is it reasonable to suppose that the precise earthly location where God gathered dust or clay to form man, is worthy of discussion?

For some, the answer to that question is…yes. For others…no.

The opinions of Biblical scholars, academic intellectuals, and authorities on history every so often can result in a collision. Their viewpoints on are influenced by, but not limited to, private interpretation, different versions of the Bible, examination of geographical facts and powerful scientific logic.

The scripture Genesis 3:23 KJV tells us "Therefore the Lord God sent him forth **from** the garden of Eden, to till the ground **from whence he was taken.**"

"The key words include, "the Lord God sent him forth **from** the garden of Eden to till the ground **from whence he was taken.**" Does sent him forth **from** the garden of Eden to "till the ground from whence he was taken" indicate that the creation of man occurred at some other location?

We could reflect on this fact. God formed man from dust or clay found at an unnamed location and it appears that He counted it wise to leave that location a mystery.

We don't know. Could the objective have been to discourage any human who may claim supremacy linked directly to God as it pertains to a racial group, the skin color, eyes, nose and hair features, or power based on where one was born. If the trinity (Father, Son, and the Holy Spirit) sparks a thought, watch this. Jesus's time on earth began after the first creation of man. In the Bible, the New Testament provides two sacred writings (Matthew and Luke) that explain the **earthly** family tree of Jesus.

Just a thought…it is likely that forever there shall be certain individuals or groups who will debate the following. Knowing the specific place where the first man was created…is…or is not important.

Could it be possible that supremacy motivated reasons are concealed in the minds of some ethnic groups when they challenge any need to examine the actual location of man's creation? Possibly some are concerned that if the truth is revealed it may not weigh in their favor.

1 Thessalonians 5:22 KJV gives this counsel. "Abstain from all appearance of evil."

Moving forward, is it reasonable to suppose that…God also gathered dust or clay at locations on the territory called The United States. With that dust or clay, along with other races, He created Native Black American people.

Please keep in mind Proverbs 4:7 KJV reminds us "Wisdom is the principal thing; therefore, get wisdom: and with all thy getting, get understanding."

Proverbs 1:2-5 KJV tells us, "To know wisdom and instruction; to perceive the words of understanding: To receive the instruction of wisdom, justice, and judgment, and equity: To give subtilty to the simple, to the young man knowledge and discretion: A wise man will hear and will increase learning; and a man of understanding shall attain unto wise counsels."

However, we must also recognize and respect the rules concerning wisdom. Isaiah 40:28 KJV "there is no searching of his understanding."

One could easily suppose that the writings mentioned above are conflicting.

Once again, we do not believe that God is looking over His shoulder.

Inquiring minds may also lift their eyes towards the hills seeking spiritual comfort. Because the exact location of God, when He created man from the dust or clay is just one of God's mysteries that calls on your confidence in Him. Said another way… at day's end your creation beliefs stand on the rock of your faith.

It is very easily to believe that more likely than not, God knew the humanity of mankind could easily justify yielding to temptation. Justifying a temptation to alter the moral intent of His kingdom. Eve and Adam.

Furthermore, we believe it is possible that the wisdom of God reasoned that the power of skin color influences and other prejudices which have gradually developed over time. Would be used as some justification or qualifying action supporting judgmental standards. The objective could be to gain supremacy over God's will.

The temptation of assuming a right to supremacy based on physical characteristics, ancestry backgrounds and a belief that they are better than others will happen. Matthew 26:41 KJV " Watch and pray, that ye enter not into temptation: the spirit indeed is willing, but the flesh is weak." Human respect and morals often drift into the mist.

Romans 12:2 KJV tells us "And be not conformed to this world: but be ye transformed by the renewing of your mind, that ye may prove what is that good, and acceptable, and perfect, will of God."

John 13:34 KJV "A new commandment I give unto you, that ye love one another; as I have loved you, that ye also love one another."

If we adopt and practice that wisdom as one of our personal codes of conduct. We can be empowered; we must stand strong and not tremble in fear simply by hearing the term…White supremacy. A power that is given.

Joshua 1:9 KJV "Have not I commanded thee? Be strong and of a good courage; be not afraid, neither be thou dismayed: for the Lord thy

God is with thee whithersoever thou goest."

The United States of America Constitution does not give unconditional sovereignty to the often-mentioned term, White supremacy.

However, that opinion was not always accepted by some United States institutions including but not limited to several State or Municipal level Governments, the United States military, and countless private organizations. There are times when the Constitution and reality can collide.

We are reminded through Ecclesiastes 3:3 KJV "To everything there is a season, and a time to every purpose under the heaven."

If you will, consider these associated facts.

A Presidential Executive Order (Number 8802) was signed by Franklin D. Roosevelt on June 25, 1941. We believe that God moved President Roosevelt to abolish discriminating employment practices by all United States of America defense organizations, federal agencies, companies, and unions engaged in war-related work. The Pentagon office building was on the front line. Such action was just another step in God's creation plan.

That display of courage was powerful. It inspired people to take their first step that led to success stories. While the course of that path required a person to navigate over slippery steppingstones. It was the beginning of a valuable journey. Remember, a journey must begin with the first step.

We are reminded of words credited to Thomas Jefferson. In the 1776, U.S. Declaration of Independence a declaration read "We hold these truths to be self-evident, that all men are created equal, that they are endowed by their Creator with certain unalienable rights. Unalienable means "impossible to take away or give up rights." All of us routinely disregard Jeffersons' intent.

History tells us that the Executive Order (Number 8802) mentioned above led to a second Presidential Executive Order (Number 9981) which was signed by Harry Truman on July 26, 1948. Again, we believe that God moved President Truman to use his Presidential powers to help abolish racial segregation within the United States Armed Forces.

There was resistance by White members of the Armed Forces. But watch this. There was resistance by Black members of the Armed Forces. Such opposition by ultra proud Native Black Americans is a topic not well known.

Sadly, certain advantages ushered in by equal opportunity rulings can easily become a handicap. Sometimes when benefits are given at no cost, no individual effort, they can become an excuse to surrender self-initiative. We are suggesting that an entitlement mentality could easily replace personal ambition.

Think of self-appointed supremacy and the awarding of academic benefits or skilled labor opportunities based social prejudices. Those value systems can collide with justice and selected fruit of the Spirit including love, peace, gentleness and goodness. Self-appointed supremacy can serve as an enabler that could prolong a privileged way of thinking powered by sometimes invisible Jim Crow values. The final goal is to satisfy a thirst to control or influence someone or something. Remember unalienable rights?

Perhaps the claim of being supreme is driven by…ethnic supremacy or racial supremacy or Tribal supremacy or religious supremacy or Nationality supremacy or social class supremacy. The supremacy labels range wide.

With that said. Once again, we submit that if the exact location of the creation of man could be uncertain for good reasons. Perhaps the brilliant wisdom of God moved Him to prevent any race from claiming supremacy…in His name. We doubt that God is looking over his shoulder.

More likely than not, God needed to make sure that nothing would take away from His desire for people to concentrate on worshiping Him.

In the Bible we can find that mortal men tend to single out several groupings of people. Of particular interest are references that identify family roots, tribes, families, human kingdoms, even skin color is talked about. But in Genesis 1:27 KJV we find, "So God created man in his own image, in the image of God created he him; male and female created he them." He made no mention of other bodily features. He only saw the kingdom of God!

Also watch this. Romans 1:14, KJV, "I am debtor both to the Greeks, and to the Barbarians; both to the wise, and to the unwise." HUM… Which group was labelled as the wise? Which group was counted as unwise?

When people have similar bodily features or come from similar geographical areas, and when they are in the majority. That can cause the same people to declare supremacy which leads to discrimination. So…we ask? Is discrimination a creation of religion or a creation of mankind?

Well, when we die. After we pass from the earthly human body into that of a non-physical spirit. Hear these questions. Will we keep our physical features? Will we keep our tendency to discriminate?

Jesus took on the human form in a male body. However, His actual skin color, hair texture, nose and eye shapes are arguably…thought provoking.

There is a tendency to create an image of Jesus that leans towards a physical appearance which represents the vision of the storyteller or recorder of history. Most often, you will see a likeness that represents the dominant race. Sometimes the ruling authority sets the standard.

Consider words in Genesis 1:27 KJV. So, God created man in his own image, in the image of God created he him; male and female created he them. Those words are at the minimum…thought provoking.

While there has been much speculation by religious scholars and scientists, a logical question could be. At what point in time and why did the different skin colors become a reason to hate even a reason to kill?

Additionally, on what authority did some institution or society justify their concept of using skin color as a basis to assume one color should be superior to another color.

Can the skin color of God affect one's inclination to be a follower of Jesus? Yes…such is possible.

Close your eyes and visualize the numerous portraits or other images that represent Jesus which you have seen. What physical image is displayed in your mind? Does what you see represent your…personal image.

Think about this. For various reasons, people worship several divine beings or supernatural powers who they believe can exert force over all things.

Ephesians 4:6 KJV. "One God and Father of all, who is above all, and through all, and in you all." Perhaps that rationale could translate to… the ultimate supremacy is commanded by God.

It is human beings that have the issues.

Furthermore, we do not believe…that God is looking over his shoulder.

Through the scriptures Jesus sent messages implying that to be a true follower of God, one's commitment cannot be conditional.

The scriptures give us many examples of unconditional commitment. In the scriptures we find the story of Shadrach, Meschach, and Abednego. The King demanded that the three men abandon their commitment to God and worship his idol.

King Nebuchadnezzar gave this command. If they failed to comply, they should be forced, while still alive into a furnace that was burning hot.

Shadrach, Meschach, and Abednego stood on one of their most important commitments to God. Exodus 20:3 KJV, "Thou shalt have no other gods before me."

We understand the power of human wants. Matthew 26:41, KJV reminds us of this…"the spirit indeed is willing, but the flesh is weak."

Pursuing certain wants without calling on God and having trust in Him is like deliberately walking on slippery steppingstones. For example. When success requires obedience with ethnic, corporate, fraternal, sorority, or peer group values that collide with God's commandments. Yielding to temptation could lead to sinking into a sea of trouble and suffering.

Matthew 14: 28-31, KJV, "And Peter answered him and said, Lord, if it be thou, bid me come unto thee on the water. And he said, Come. And when Peter was come down out of the ship, he walked on the water, to go to Jesus. But the threating waves caused Peter to become afraid; and beginning to sink, he cried, saying, Lord, save me. And immediately Jesus stretched forth his hand, and caught him, and said unto him, O thou of little faith, wherefore didst thou doubt?"

Ecclesiastes 12:13, KJV. "Let us hear the conclusion of the whole matter: Fear God and keep his commandments: for this is the whole duty of man."

We also encourage you to pause for a moment and focus on this motivating viewpoint "The journey of a thousand miles begins with a single step." That advice is inspired by words found in Chapter 64 of Dao De Jing, an ancient Chinese writing.

As we make the journey through life. We will come across many slippery steppingstones or challenges hidden in our paths. There shall be some happiness – some sadness - some success and some failure. To everything there is a season, and a time

Through sacrifices by your ancestors who helped to build this Country. Through your birthright. By shedding your blood in military and work in civilian service you have earned the right to share benefits of "Life, Liberty, and the pursuit of Happiness" declared in the United States Declaration of Independence. Redirect all energy that is powered by rejection. Make rejection one of the power sources of your strength. Choose your mentors wisely. "He that walketh with wise men shall be wise. but a companion of fools shall be destroyed." Proverbs 13:20 KJV.

Keep in mind that success is not only measured by you, but by others who are judging you. It is likely that a success assessment decided by self-anointed supremacist will not weigh in your favor.

Your life's success demands the courage to…begin with a single step.

2 Thessalonians 3:10, KJV tells us: "For even when we were with you, this we commanded you, that if any would not work…neither should he eat."

We ask you to pause for a minute and think about these important facts.

Researching the word Native, one definition tells us that Native is used to define a person who has not migrated from somewhere else. To go further, Native identifies a person who was born in a specific Nation, State, City or similar place.

But watch this. Native is a word often used in a way intended to color the entire Black race in a negative way. For some when they use the word Native…it implies a poorly educated, morally corrupt person. A person dependent on charity, guidance, and knowledge of the ruling class.

When used with a wicked intent, the word Native could be correctly described as a "Dog Whistle".

For the record, dog whistle is a term that may seem innocent. But it is a code word that contains unspoken or covert meanings. Dog Whistles support the thoughts of a particular group without drawing much attention.

Sadly, because Dog Whistle words are subject to many opinions. The message bearer can easily wash their hands and hide from any guilt or pain that the word may bring.

Think of a shadow. It requires some another object as a source of energy. You can see a shadow moving on the ground, but that shadow cannot be touched, it leaves no footprint nor makes any sound as it moves. Watch this. The shadow has power…yet it cannot produce a its' own shadow.

Nevertheless, a shadow can control or influence one's state of mind. That influence can be driven by several factors.

Among the factors which give strength to a shadow is a fear of superstition and a fear of events that may seem beyond the laws of nature. Fear can lead to accepting controlling rules that may not be in your best interest.

Do not surrender and be controlled by a shadow coming from one who claims a self-appointed supremacy.1-Timothy 4:7 KJV tells us "But refuse profane and old wives' fables and exercise thyself rather unto godliness."

We count it wise to leave it to your mental strength and self-discipline to make sound judgements as it pertains to how shadows affect your life.

Some people who reside in the "hood" use that word to define their neighborhood with emotions that voice a very passionate pride. However, it is not uncommon for non-residents to use "hood" to identify a poor, crime ridden neighborhood. Not a preferred place for residence.

For this writing…hood is exposed as another dog whistle word. Think about the behavior traits implied when someone is called a…hoodlum.

Hear this. Consider the 7 shadows that often linger over any neighborhood affectionately referred to by some as the "Hood."

1. The "hood" is challenged by a practice called redlining. Redlining amounts to the intentional lowering in value of houses and the quality of other services. Control of the transport system can restrict certain people to a segregated area. That includes a tendency to flood certain areas with used vehicles. Often one will have limited travel capability because of used car mechanical challenges. The burdens associated with redlining trap some people into lifelong existence under unfavorable conditions.

2. Countless people suffer from not being considered for higher

academic opportunities or employment advancement. Simply because they are judged based on presumed traits or morals for one reason. Their "hood" zip codes.

3. The "hood" is challenged by the lack of adequate fresh food stores. Often referred to as food deserts.

4. The "hood" is challenged by too many families that are not privileged to have the mother and father present and the benefit of both serving as active maintainers / leaders of the household.

5. The "hood" is challenged because many family members and friends are in prison.

6. The "hood" is challenged by the absence of a lot of positive male and female role models.

7. Perhaps by accepting residing in the "hood" as an unchangeable destiny, that person contributes to or prolongs the evil of discrimination. In doing so, that same one surrenders to being dominated by self-anointed supremist?

How long…how long…will Black people accept or suffer the empty feeling of being without hope? How long will there be a tendency to lean on fake passionate pride? Too often fake passionate pride becomes an excuse to accept living in the "hood" as a part of life that is beyond a person's control.

Said another way, some people accept living in the "hood" as a pre-ordained destiny. Often, influenced by that mystifying shadow called "the man" has them financially and emotionally…locked in!

To anyone willing to listen we humbly request that you pray and call on the last of your energy. Never take any action that will help your enemy grow stronger.

We believe that deep within our soul there is a powerful emotional calling to take our place in history. We understand…we do not, we can't overlook the connection to Africa. But…we are who we are. Native Black Americans.

Some pretend to embrace that blemished racial name, African American. Some accept this new racial creation, Native Black American. Think of John 15:16 KJV "Ye have not chosen me, but I have chosen you."

It is always good and pleasant to be a member of the in-crowd.

However, it would not be wise if one turned against their own spirituality and personal values simply to be identified as African American. Peer pressure, trying to fit in at all costs, can lead destructive behavior. Matthew 26:41 KJV tells us to "Watch and pray, that ye enter not into temptation: the spirit indeed is willing, but the flesh is weak. The challenge is challenging.

If being accepted into the wrong in-crowd is not in your best interest, stay faithful to God. Do not turn to the left or right if sinful acts are included.

Consider the wisdom explained in the KJV of Luke 8: 22 – 23 -24 - 25.

22. "Now it came to pass on a certain day, that he went into a ship with his disciples: and he said unto them, let us go over unto the other side of the lake."

23. "But as they sailed, he fell asleep: and there came down a storm of wind on the lake; and they were filled with water and were in jeopardy."

24 And they came to him, and awoke him, saying, Master, master, we perish. Then he arose and rebuked the wind and the raging of the water: and they ceased, and there was a calm.

25 And he said unto them, where is your faith?

One lesson that can be learned is if we know the in-crowd direction is not the right path. We must have the strength and courage to shake the toxic soil from our shoes and travel forward on the right path. Let us work with a stubborn attitude to improve life for ourselves. If for nothing else…fueling a new racial illumination for our descendants that is not blemished.

Perhaps something to consider is this. If one is standing still while others are moving forward. If one is satisfied or comfortable with waiting for crumbs to fall from the king's table. If one accepts the suffering and the disgrace of being classified as a national nobody. If one accepts African American, a national title that will impact your quality of life. Then we lose.

Sometimes travelling on the right path can make you look back and question your decisions. You may say the burden is too heavy. Keep in mind Psalm 55:22 KJV. "Cast thy burden upon the Lord, and he shall sustain thee: he shall never suffer the righteous to be moved."

Just to be accepted by the in-crowd. Does it really make sense to take the wrong but feel-good path which you know will take you in the wrong direction?

Psalm 84:10 KJV tells us "I had rather be a doorkeeper in the house of my God, than to dwell in the tents of wickedness." Is the in-crowd worth it?

Deuteronomy 8:2 KJV "And thou shalt remember all the way which the Lord thy God led thee these forty years (**we could say 400 years**) in the wilderness, to humble thee, and to prove thee, to know what was in thine heart, whether thou keep his commandments"

With that said. Are you sick and tired of being sick and tired of having your national race identity changed 7 times during…give or take… at 12-year intervals? Come on! Stand up and fight, it is called racial cleansing. If you continue reading this writing those 7 name changes will be revealed.

Pseudo is derivative of a Greek word "psedues" which describes something that is false or lying. Pseudo has the power to persuade a person to believe that something is true. However, that "something" is in fact…not true. Identifying people who were born on the soil of the United States, we are talking about Native Black Americans. Identifying them as African Americans is surely a pseudo moment. African American is misleading.

We encourage any Native Black American who is starving for their own National racial identity to make a sacrifice. Go on a Daniel Fast and refuse to eat the crumbs which fall from the table of those who claim the right or the privilege to assign a name to your race. If we surrender to the will of God, we will rise successful. If we continue seeking to be a part of any race that will accept us, we surrender to the power of self-appointed supremacy.

Pause and think about that term "the man." Who gives "the man" authority? What makes one surrender just by hearing these words… "the man"?

Is it some shadow blocking the light needed for one's vision causing an unconscious fear? Could one be thinking, I have a fear of becoming free.

The reality is…submission based on fear gives confidence to those who feel empowered to exercise self-appointed supremacy over you.

Joshua 5:13. KJV tells us. "And it came to pass, when Joshua was by Jericho, that he lifted up his eyes and looked, and, behold, there stood a man over against him with his sword drawn in his hand: and Joshua went unto him, and said unto him, Art thou for us, or for our adversaries?"

I have heard it said. The man keeps me down. The man stopped my promotion. The man stopped my pursuit of seeking education. The man creates guidelines that affect my ability to be a good father or mother. The list is sadly long. Ask that mysterious man that you seem to idolize, perhaps worship. Are you for us…or against us?

With that said, in some situations, if you pause for a moment and look into a mirror. The image of the "man" may be surprising. It just might be you, that is holding you back.

While researching the word indigenous, one definition tells us that indigenous applies when a person naturally exists in a place or Country, rather than arriving from another location. Indigenous talks to something homegrown or occurring naturally on a specific land mass. While going over the word indigenous. Clearly, indigenous includes human beings.

We put forward a conclusion that Native Black Americans born on the

United States of America soil are indigenous citizens.

Furthermore, is also not unusual to find that the words…race and ethnicity…are often confused with one another.

While exploring the word Ethnic, one definition tells us that ethnicity can be influenced by several factors. Those elements tend to be defined by place of birth, ancestry, physical appearance, hair styles, language or dialect, food types and its preparation, clothing, shoes, boots or the lack of any footwear, headgear, society and social group rules, religious beliefs and rituals, accepted traditions and customs, source of education, music favorites, and shared cultural values.

Without hesitation we argue that many Ethnic traits linked to Native Black Americans, were created on the soil of the United States of America.

Race in terms of human labeling generally refers to a person's skin color, the color of hair and is it curly, wavy, or straight, eye color and shapes and facial shapes. Thinking about the realities of today's world, changing climatic conditions and interracial genetic mixing. The physical looks of many humans do not follow racial cookie cutter standards as in the past.

Historical storylines try to persuade anyone willing to listen that it was in the year of 1619, when Africans first set foot on North America soil.

That may have been the year when a group of African people who had been captured or purchased were unloaded from a sailing ship onto United States soil. Those humans were set apart to be sold to the highest bidder their ill-fated destiny was…to serve as slaves.

However, be on your guard. The dates as it pertains to the first Africans to set foot on North American soil has a high chance of being inaccurate.

The story may have been reported as seen through the narrow-focused eyes of history keepers. Perhaps the recording of history was controlled or influenced to reinforce supremacy. Perhaps diminish the importance of any Black people who had set foot on the land many years before the United States declared Independence.

Footprints left by Black people making positive impacts on United States history cannot not be erased. Sadly, the robbing of individual and group history during slavery did leave another footprint. The imprint of bigotry standing on the shoulders of many Black Americans has caused a lingering challenge. The qualities needed to stick together and support each other as a race has been severely weakened.

This fact is submitted just as a matter of interest. The clearly visible name on the hull of that ship which brought captured or purchased Africans to Yorktown in 1619 was…the White Lion. Hum…ironic we dare say.

We point to one documented account from history which tells us that a Black African man traveled with Ponce de León to the land that would become the United States. Ponce de León was a trail blazer who explored foreign areas. In 1513 he led an expedition searching for the Fountain of Youth in Florida. A difference of 100 years plus when compared to 1619.

Psalm 90:10, KJV tells us "The days of our years are threescore years and ten; and if by reason of strength they be fourscore years."

While there may be a bit of dispute as it pertains to factors concerning the accuracy of when a generation begins and ends. Pause and reflect on "threescore years and ten; and if by reason of strength they be fourscore years." Using the Biblical figure eighty (80) as a creative touch point. Let us suppose the figure 80 represents a generation or an estimated time in the average life cycle of men and women.

If we use the years 1619 and 2019 as touch points. If we employ a process or set of rules to be followed in calculations and other mathematical solving scenarios or if you will, a set of rules. The year 2019, minus the year 1619 equals 400 years. 400 years divided by an average of 80 years can equal, give or take, 5 generations.

The intended point is this. 5 generations have passed. Therefore, if we can agree that at a minimum, 5 generations of Black People have been born on North American soil. That marks 5 generations for Native Black Americans.

We give all respect to those departed Africa as captives. The same humans were loaded into ships as property. Sailing through the Atlantic triangle trade system they arrived in North America as slaves.

Again, there is no denial that Native Black American people have genetic connections with the African Continent. However, as it pertains to a large percent of the Native Black American people. Identifying an exact place of origin and a specific family group in Africa is a challenge. However, for some inquiring minds the search seems a sensible effort. Absolute success can be compared to soaring with the currents of the wind. We do not know where the wind came from, and we do not know its journey's end.

For 5 plus generations while wandering through a wilderness of trials and hardships. God has blessed Native Black Americans by never leaving us or turning away from us. He gave us wisdom, courage, and a strong will to win. We shall forever pursue a credible national name that accurately identifies Black people who were born in the United States of America.

After over 5 plus generations of interracial sex, sometimes only one partner agreed. Other times both partners agreed. The result is...the blood or genetics flowing through the veins of a high percent of Black people born in the United States, is eternally integrated with many different races. The result...a new creation, a new race. Native Black American.

Personal opinions about scriptures involving race and ethnicity can be a subject of intense discussion. Some views conflict with the spoken intent of God. From time to time in Biblical writings, you can find race, skin color or place of birth used as a reason to deal with people in different ways.

Considering the will of God. Considering exact meaning of the words Native and Indigenous. Considering language in the Constitution of the United States of America. We stand strong with noble courage and proclaim that Black people born in the United States for 5 generations plus. We have without question, earned the right to enjoy the freedom of this new creation...**Native Black Americans.**

One definition of refugee: Someone who is seeking place of safety or asylum. An individual who has left his or her native country and is unwilling or unable to return to it. Fear of persecution, ethnic cleansing, being exiled or threatened with death. For religious problems, politics and war.

One definition of immigrant: Immigrants are inspired to leave their countries Some reasons may include a desire to change one's quality of life, better job opportunities, family reunification or marriage. Weather associated migration, religious freedom, escape from an environment soaked in bigotry, or suffering natural disasters.

Neither of the above terms can be correctly used to describe a Native Black American. We are who we are, indigenous and native North Americans.

Numbers 13, KJV, 31-33, tell us that during the early religious era, the prophet Moses sent spies into the land of Canaan.

31. "But the men that went up with him said, we are not able to go up against the people; for they are stronger than we."

33. "And there we saw the giants, the sons of Anak, we were in our own sight as grasshoppers, and so we were in their sight."

The opinions of the men who were sent, report several points of view which could be described as imperfect judgements.

1. God had promised to grant ownership of the new land. He always keeps his promises. It certainly appears that they had more confidence in their own surveys than in the promise of God.

2. It is possible the spies' offered opinions that by design gave the wrong impression. Did their mind's imagination result in giving up their self-respect based on a fear of implied supremacy. "The man."

3. Ruling groups and individuals are generally clever at enforcing and reinforcing their self-centered justification to claim supremacy.

A self-fulfilling prophecy is when you describe what you think will happen in the future. Sometimes your own behavior causes that prophecy to happen.

Some people exploit fear, financial power, political power, judicial power, and power associated with employment opportunities. Let us not forget the advantages of an important name or symbol indicating a rank, office, or profession. Let us not forget superior weapons and presumed supremacy.

Driven by our own fear, how much longer will we cause our future generations to suffer this racial identity (African American). A tag that can point to many people from many Countries. Have the courage to stand strong with noble courage raise the dignity flag: Native Black American.

Keep in mind that in the past, constantly changing the race name of American Black people was nothing more a controlling or domination tool.

A weathervane, also called a windvane, is a gadget mounted at the highest point of a structure quite often a barn. It rotates or changes direction in response to the wind. Wind vanes are generally decorated with images representing eagles, rosters, horses. Often you will see an arrow with markings indicating four directions, the North, East, South or West. Again, it will point in a direction according to wind influences.

To anyone…who has accepted what seems to be one too many racial name changes for Black people who were born in the United States. Are you guided by a moral windvane…that is pointing in the wrong direction?

The question is, why would anyone timidly accept becoming slave to some racial identity that changes with the wind? Think of surrendering without resistance and moving in any direction that the wind vane points. Especially if that direction is not in one's best interest. The question is, why not control of your own windvane? Where is our thirst for a self-driven dignity?

Black people born in the United States who bow and obediently answer to the racial identity African American must consider adjusting their windvane.

If for no other reason, empower the generations that come after you with the opportunity to demand recognition of a dignified national identity void of any uncertainty. Brothers and sisters stop roaming through life without claiming a genuine Nationality. Native Black American!

Keep this in mind. African immigrants and their descendants sometimes give the impression that they are less than eager to count Native Black Americans as authentic Africans.

That leads us to ask this question. How long, how long will some display an eagerness to take a knee before what could be seen as a supremacist idol. We are talking about the words African American. We are talking about the shadowy worship of stuff like clothing and hair styles associated with the African sphere of influences. Other than music can anybody give worthy examples of Africans imitating Native Black American influences?

That is especially true when the deceptive mask worn by many Africans is removed. The mask conceals their tendency to count Native Black Americans as Africans…only when it is convenient. It is also not unusual for African immigrants to consider that their Country of origin has a right to hold supremacy over Native Black Americans. African Supremacist?

We have stated over and over, there is no denial that Native Black Americans share, although it is fuzzy, a genetic and cultural association with somebody located someplace on the African Continent. On the other hand, Native Black Americans are knit into the United States culture. Native Black Americans also have definable blood lines and natural or by-law family connections within the United States borders. A new race is born.

Notwithstanding, as we ponder the need for change. Let us always remember that The United States of America is the sovereign Country to which Native Black Americans owe allegiance. Let us always remember we have earned the benefits associated with that valuable allegiance.

Just intended to serve as a quiet nudge, see the following excerpt

---

Constitution of the United States of America Preamble

We the People of the United States, in Order to form a more perfect Union, establish Justice, insure domestic Tranquility, provide for the common defence, promote the general Welfare, and secure the Blessings of Liberty to ourselves and our Posterity, do ordain and establish this Constitution for the United States of America.

When considering the numerous documents that shepherded the founding of the United States of America. Two of the principal foundation documents are the Declaration of Independence and the National Constitution.

While the people involved in drafting process of those significant documents agreed to a variety of strategies, objectives, and goals. There can be no doubt that the document drafters had to be influenced by private judgements. Let us not overlook ethnic. cultural and governing influences.

There are some who believe that a large percentage of the language in the US Constitution may have been written with only European Colonizers in mind. Humans counted as three fifths of a person may not a been a priority.

Come with us if you will. Let us take a quick look at The United States Constitution specifically the Three-Fifth Clause.

The Three-fifths Compromise was an agreement reached during the 1787 United States Constitutional Convention. It focused on the counting of slaves in determining a State's total population. A concern was, in certain States. Too many slaves could tilt the scales.

This Compromise would affect the number of seats in the House of Representatives and how much each state would pay in taxes. A residual effect was it reduced the value of each Black man, woman and child to three-fifths of a human being. This gave birth to the "one drop" theory.

Does this represent a conflict with spirit of God's word? Genesis 1:27 KJV. "God created man in his own image. Was Jesus three-fifths of a man?

But watch this…Free Blacks were not subject to the compromise, and each was counted as one full person. Hum…That seems to present a selective interpretation of the Three-fifths Compromise law.

For many years. The Three-Fifths Compromise was used to justify various levels of discrimination.

1 Peter 2:15 KJV tells us "For so is the will of God, that with well doing ye may put to silence the ignorance of foolish men."

With time, the Three-fifths Compromise was repealed by Article 1, Section 2, Clause 3. Section 2 of the Fourteenth Amendment to the United States Constitution.

There were individuals tasked with reviewing language in the USA Constitution. The solution was to make actual population numbers the basis of apportioning the seats in the House of Representatives.

This included rules deciding matters involving tax liability among the states.

Because of this change, the Constitution mandated that a census would be taken every ten years to establish the population of each state within the United States.

We want to circle back to the "one drop" theory. A theory which some pretended to be set by nature. However, it was an attempt by mankind to make one race superior to another. Anytime there is evidence of anyone having any African person anyplace in their family tree. That person shall be classified as having at least one drop of African blood. In the eyes of some, one drop of African blood makes that person impure or blemished.

As a result of that judgement, one could be in danger of being deprived of valuable privileges during their entire life. One could be deprived of privileges granted by the United States of America Declaration of Independence.

Remember these words. "We hold these truths to be self-evident, that all men are created equal, that they are endowed by their Creator with certain unalienable Rights, that among these are Life, Liberty and the pursuit of Happiness."

Even among Native Black Americans we find it interesting that the color of one's skin has an impact. There are judgements and treatments driven by very light complected and very dark complected skin colors.

Research has validated this point of interest. In this day and time, the world has many people who have mixed blood flowing through their veins.

Let us pray for those who have a thirst to prolong or favor the "one drop" theory. One could say that such philosophy reveals shallow self-confidence.

We reflect once again on this wisdom and this patience. Luke 23:34 KJV "Then said Jesus, Father, forgive them; for they know not what they do."

Remember Genesis 2:7 KJV tells us "And the Lord God formed man of the dust of the ground and breathed into his nostrils the breath of life; and man became a living soul."

Since God created man and breathed life into him. One can have faith that His creations did not include persons condemned to be three-fifths of a human. One can also have faith that God did not discriminate in His creations by separating races based on a "one drop" theory.

The supremacy of God cannot be successfully challenged! God shall have his way.

At the end of the day, we wonder. Could African American be a deliberate intent to leave out or limit the Native Black American rights as beneficiaries of their Constitutional rights? We will address that later.

We submit this thought for consideration. If there was an evil intent by the unjust. With the rising of the sun, evil has begun to fade into the darkness.

Zephaniah 3:5 KJV. "The just Lord is in the midst thereof; he will not do iniquity: every morning doth he bring his judgment to light, he faileth not; but the unjust knoweth no shame."

As stated earlier, we do not believe that God is looking over his shoulder.

CHAPTER TWO
The Fall Chapter

Pledge of Allegiance

I pledge allegiance to the flag of the United States of America, and to the republic for which it stands, one nation under God, indivisible, with liberty and justice for all.

There has long been debate as to who created the current version of the Pledge of Allegiance. Perhaps it was Francis Bellamy, perhaps James Upham.

To kind of unpack the Pledge of Allegiance we offer the following.

In the beginning the words innocently read "my flag". However, an amendment was deemed necessary when it became apparent that some immigrants and some refugees were making a pledge. But, in a deceptive way. They were pledging allegiance to the Country of their birth.

A change modified the Pledge to read, "I pledge allegiance to the flag of the United States of America, and to the republic for which it stands."

Think of Joshua 5:13 KJV "Art thou for us, or for our adversaries?"

"One Nation under God indivisible" referred to actions and conditions linked to the Civil War. There was a collective desire and efforts to welcome those States in rebellion back because they were valuable assets to the United States of America. The freedom to worship God was a mutually held value. A desire for religious freedom from European Countries was a factor in framing the Declaration of Independence for the United States of America.

"Liberty and Justice for all" could relate to Amos 5:24, KJV, which reminds us "But let judgment run down as waters, and righteousness as a mighty stream." In other words, if justice and morally right is accepted and practiced according to the will of God. The outcome will be like refreshing streams of water coming down, relaxing the body and mind.

Galatians 3:28, KJV. Shares "There is neither Jew nor Greek, there is neither bond nor free, there is neither male nor female: for ye are all one in Christ Jesus." Liberty, justice and happiness for all of God's people.

Therefore, we submit that driven by the importance of justifying citizenship and dedication to our Country. The Pledge of Allegiance is a privilege and responsibility. For at a minim of 5 generations, there is strong evidence that Native Black Americans have earned the privilege to place their right hand over the heart and pledge allegiance to the United States of America flag.

There is one flag that represents this, Nation. That flag is the symbol of the United States of America which represents all who are citizens, When we reflect on the importance of the Stars and Stripes this question comes to mind. Are you with us or against us?

Matthew 6:24 KJV provides this accurate wisdom. "No man can serve two masters: for either he will hate the one and love the other; or else he will hold to the one and despise the other."

Please keep in mind. Native Black Americans are citizens of the United States. Although most of our ancestors were viewed as material goods to be bought and sold. One could say that they were chattel. However, today we are indigenous or native citizens. Let it be known that we have contributed with our life and labor to the commerce and defense of our motherland, the United States of America.

We are proud to be Americans and in view of the alternative possibilities…we count it a blessing.

Despite certain social justice failures, the United States of America is very much a desired destination. Without question it is a rewarding Nation.

While the fundamental concept for founding the United States of America as a sovereign Nation was a vision of people from Europe. Native Black Americans contributed by joining in the fight for its independence and ongoing National defense, assisted in building the infrastructure, contributed to developing a strong economic strength, added to the cultural and religious enrichment.

We make this statement. Even when considering the brutal past and continuing mistreatment of Native Black Americans. In fact, we really should include most communities throughout the world. There remain many good reasons to walk away from African American, a blemished title. One is the title can legally be used by people from many different races, by people from many different countries. We are citizens of the United States.

Bigotry or prejudice against anyone purely because they belong to another race, or some of their physical appearance is not like yours… is wrong. Since we were all created in the image of God, since His race is unknown, since no one has ever seen Him. Should race centered bigotry or prejudice also be directed against God?

It is necessary that we think rationally as we pursue racial recognition and not drown in the tears of our anger. We must resist becoming overcome with emotions that demand vengeance. Vengeance is mine, said the Lord.

Admittedly, sometimes vengeance happens, but the satisfaction of getting revenge will not last long. Philippians 3:13 KJV counsels us, "forget those things which are behind and reach forth for those things which are ahead."

We encourage dignified Native Black Americans to follow Ephesians 6:10-11 KJV. "Put on the whole amour of God that ye may be able to stand against the wiles of the devil." Do the opposite of what may be expected. Show a level of mental and moral strength that will survive wicked oppression.

That appeal is also inspired in a declaration. Deuteronomy 31:6 (KJV) "Be strong and of a good courage, fear not, nor be afraid of them: for the Lord thy God, he it is that doth go with thee; he will not fail thee, nor forsake thee."

We must use wisdom, and iron will as we fight for an unblemished racial name. However, one should seek deserved justice by fishing from the **RIGHT** side of the ship. Here is where the idea for that comment came from.

John 21:4-5-6 KJV tells us, "But when the morning was now come, Jesus stood on the shore: but the disciples knew not that it was Jesus. Then Jesus saith unto them, Children, have ye any meat? They answered him, No. And he said unto them, **Cast the net on the <u>right side</u> of the ship, and ye shall find**. They cast therefore, and now their catch was plentiful."

We believe that to achieve the desired racial recognition it is necessary to symbolically fish from the right side of a ship.

Also keep in mind that as United States of America native citizens we must stand on the foundations laid by God. There are also certain United States laws and traditions that we need to embrace and comply with.

Circling back again, there are people who have expressed a preference to celebrate Juneteenth as opposed to July 4 or Independence Day.

July 4 or Independence Day celebrates the Declaration of Independence by the thirteen colonies from Great Britain in 1776. In this setting Independence Day recognizes birth of the United States of America.

Some point to Juneteenth as a time to celebrate the freeing of slaves but then there is a shade of gray. Juneteenth spoke mainly to slaves in Galveston Texas. It seems that celebrating Juneteenth Day for all slaves may lack some depth. In the eyes of many, the stated reasoning is muddy. We should encourage everyone to fish from the right side of the ship.

Void of any intent to disrespect the right of anybody who celebrates Juneteenth. Could it be that a National Juneteenth celebration is not valued by a wide range of Native Black Americans? A possibility may be that interest in Juneteenth is regional and does not represent the best national interests of all citizens of the United States. Mark 3:25 KJV. "And if a house be divided against itself, that house cannot stand."

Matthew 6:24 KJV. "No man can serve two masters: for either he will hate the one and love the other; or else he will hold to the one and despise the other."

Could an alternative be? Respect and celebrate the 4th of July. Find another day to celebrate the signing of the Emancipation Proclamation. Possibly that will strengthen the honoring of, respect for, and acceptance of Native Black American as a legitimate race.

Needed are National holidays that contribute to and benefit the unification of the entire United States of America community. Yes, we know that rule is not true today. Every race wants a day of respect that serves their interest.

Perhaps tricky people who claim to support Juneteenth really do not pray for or hope for unification. Maybe they want to drive a wedge between Native Black Americans and other Americans. We ask you to think about it. Can divide and conquer tactics cut both ways. Like a two-edged sword.

There is a downside to worshipping Juneteenth in place of celebrating the valuable Declaration of Independence by the United States of America.

We have witnessed this fact. People who consider themselves to be supreme understand that if they can control confusion, they can control the outcome. For the record, that belief is not set aside only for racial issues.

We are reminded of 1 Corinthians 14:33 KJV. That wisdom tells us "God is not the author of confusion, but of peace."

Again, we must fish from the RIGHT side of the ship.

A Native Black American named Frederick Douglass was inspired by oppressive events and became an advocate for freedom, an orator, a writer, and statesman. His name given at birth was Frederick Augustus Washington Bailey. After escaping from the chains of slavery, he was influenced by words in a poem and changed his last name to Douglass.

Of interest, Frederick Douglass's birth was the result of a relationship involving an African salve woman and a European man.

Looking once again at the law of evolution. Hear ye, hear ye. Yet another reminder that the blood or genetics flowing through the veins of a high percent of Black people born in the United States. It has been eternally mixed with the blood or genes linked to many different racial groups.

Frederick Douglass shared this wisdom in a quote. "Power concedes nothing without a demand. It never did and it never will."

He also gave this reflection. "The limits of tyrants are prescribed by the endurance of those whom they oppress."

We are aware of self-appointed supremist who see the average Black America as nothing more that simplistic, uneducated and morally corrupt.

Unfortunately, some Native Black Americans do portray themselves as simplistic, uneducated and morally corrupt. Some have an entitlement mentality. For example, have you ever heard this born to lose outlook? "Why vote, because my vote does not count". We feel certain that you have also heard these words or excuses. "The man stopped me from achieving something and the man messed me up."

Hear this fact. For the record, no race is exempt from the characteristics of simplistic, uneducated and morally corrupt. 1 John 1:8 KJV, "If we say that we have no sin, we deceive ourselves, and the truth is not in us."

We simply cannot surrender to those who believe that one race is born superior to another based solely on differences in skin color, the hair texture, the shape of one's eyes, and ethnicity. Let us not overlook other things that are different such as where a person was born and language.

We shall follow the wisdom found in Philippians 3:14 KJV, "I press toward the mark for the prize of the high calling."

Native Black Americans must reach for the mark of higher dignity, higher academic successes, higher business ownership, higher level of craftsman skills, and higher military leadership positions.

Ebonics is a combination of the words Ebony and phonics. It is a language that is by design different from standard American English. Give up this Ebonics language which at the end of the day, only creates a self-imposed glass ceiling.

There are people who take pride if they prove skilled when expressing themselves in Ebonics. Have you ever heard anybody say…Ebonics represents Native Black Americans pride? That is a subject for much debate.

Unfortunately, some surrender to peer pressure believing that speaking in the Ebonics tongue is necessary for acceptance in certain settings or situations. For the record, let it be known that there is a silent majority who…do not value Ebonics talk.

We submit that one should not attempt to integrate any unique trait, or action into Native Black American values that is harmful to the race image.

Think about this fact. English is the official language for the United States. English is also a language preferred by many people worldwide.

We must always take the first step in a journey to lift our own race. We must set very high standards for every Native Black American. Our journey should be measured with this in mind. "As far as the east is from the west." If you set out traveling from the West towards the East. You will find that the journey will last forever. You cannot settle for just achieving success. You cannot settle for; I did my best. Your best is not good enough.

Motivated by fear of rebellion by strong willed slaves and a move to suggest that the master has supremacy over their property. Slave owners saw it necessary to use divide and conquer tactics.

Sadly, many Black slaves in America fell victim to a technique called brainwashing which is a process of repeating certain ideas or beliefs over and over. Until the ideas or beliefs are accepted as true or agree with.

Many Black slave gave in to the very effective divide and conquer tactics. Unfortunately, the results of divide and conquer plots can still be found within the Native Black American way of life…Sometimes, we avoid putting ourselves out there when we could provide help to Native Black Americans.

As it pertains to most States or local governments, Black slaves were forbidden to gather in large groups unless controlled by a White overseer. Sometimes the exception was during Sunday worship services. However, behind the pulpit was a large painting of God who had European features.

Countless African slaves, lost respect for other slaves particularly those of different tribal origins. In fact, a strong dislike among Africans was encouraged by slave owners and overseers. Lost was self-respect. Lost was ethnic mixing. Lost is respect by Black people for other Black people if one's skin color was different. You can see it in today's Black culture.

A vital factor in the institution's divide and conquer strategy involved a scheme to confuse just who the Black Americans were. In the past, the strategy included constantly changing the race designation for Black people born in the United States. Devalue their cultural values and family lineage.

That model came close to successfully stripping Native Black Americans of any long-standing racial identity. But God placed a ram in the bush.

The Lord works in mysterious ways. The number 7 is a figure that signifies completion or perfection. After 6 different racial names; Slave, Negro, Nigger, Colored, Afro American, and Black People.

We now have achieved completion or perfection in our pursuit of an unblemished name. This 7th name is Native Black American.

As shared earlier there are indicators that a very large number African people and their descendants do not respect Black people who were born on the soil of the Americas or the Caribbean.

So, among other questions we ask.

What's in a name? Why would a parent give a name to a child that could have a negative impact on their future opportunities? Yes, that does happen. The slippery slope could be this. People who have power over the future of your child may not share your high opinion for certain names. Rejection, discrimination based solely on a name is a fact of life.

At the end of the day does the value added by satisfying the needs of the person giving a name…add value to the person who must live with that name?

It was a common practice to bury slaves in unmarked graves to weaken family ancestry footprints. Families were broken up by selling the father or the mother or the children to another owner. The new owner normally had a plantation located far away. Divide and conquer.

Over approximately 5 generations the so-called official race designation applicable to Native Black Americans has changed more than any other race on earth! Why? Today, the exact race naming for Black people born in the United States of America continues as a subject of uncertainty.

If you will, consider this. You can see the power of wind moving the United States flag about. You can also feel the effects of the wind on your body. Again…you do not know exactly where the wind came from, nor do know exactly where it is going. Maybe the Native Black American title has been moving through time, traveling on the wind. Its destiny was to touch down here and now. We believe consistent with the will of God.

Its destiny was to touch down here and now. We believe consistent with the will of God.

Some people are willing to simply to be politically correct. Others have different motives. Both have assumed that they have certain rights and without permission, they have incorrectly attempted to assign the very misleading name "African American" to Native Black Americans. No thanks.

Ecclesiastes 7:1 KJV, "A good name is better than precious ointment." Native born Black Americans want to see fulfillment of that scripture. Now!

There exist many attempts to justify accepting the title African American. Some are well-intentioned, some self-serving, some may fit into a "they tried hard" category. Some rely on a claim of hereditary connections to Africa. That can be like standing on a slippery slope when the blowing wind is strong. Other than wide-ranging Country possibilities it can be difficult to identify clear-cut geographical connections within Africa. Identifying a family connection in a specific city, township, or neighborhood, on the African Continent is at a minimum, challenging.

There is no dispute that Black Americans have hereditary associations traceable to someplace on the African Continent. However, over several centuries our spoken language, genetics, our culture and a lot of other stuff has changed. We have developed into a new class Associate the words "new beginning" with the biblical number eight (8) in mind.

To those who seem to have a certain pride in identifying with the title "African American" hear this contrast that is often silent.

Immigrants from Africa to the United States, as a rule view the place of birth linked to past family generations as their own native land or country. But Native Black Americans cannot break off this reality. While it is often silent many decline to self-classify as African American.

How long…how long. Will an unknown number of Native Black Americans appear to be consumed with migrating their racial identity back onto the shores of African? Especially when Africans are often unwelcoming. The reality is…Native Black Americans will be identified as foreigners…not as Africans coming home. An United States of America passport is required.

Surely the following statement will be disputed by some. There are clear-cut differences between Native Black Americans and African people.

Language or words used to communicate are different. Worship behaviors are in general terms, different. Where food selections similarities exist the preparation process is typically different. The dress codes are different. Man and woman equality views are as a rule different. It goes on and on.

How long…will North American Black people accept any assigned racial grouping that is listed on an application just to have a racial identity to associate with? If the selection options ignore Native Black American and if you have the courage, why not enter the word "other".

After 5 plus generations of being native and indigenous to North America, how long…how long will we allow ourselves to be held back by the iron chains of colonialism? How long will we allow some institution or someone else to give Native American Black people a false National racial Identity. We publicly announce…no longer!

Keep your eyes on the prize. We are suggesting a new National racial Identity that will be accepted and seen as worthy of great honor. Native Black American is a new racial Identity that shall be accepted and recognized by all cultures…reaching throughout the entire world.

No institution, no individual, no other race has the right or obligation to serve as architects to make this change real. This calling is essentially asking Native Black Americans to stand up. Add force to correcting our racial identity and therefore, enhance the dignity of our descendants.

We are reminded of a proverb from the Latin tongue, the Italic language that was used in Ancient Rome. Novus ordo seclorum. Translated we find, "New order of the ages"

Keep this wisdom in mind.

Matthew 6:24 KJV, presents sound wisdom that continues valid in the present day. "No man can serve two masters: for he will hate one and love the other." Does that thinking apply to those who hold dual citizenship or Nationality?

We will pause for just one moment to identify some of the African Countries who have made significant footprints on the United States of America soil.

Without any planned exclusion or indication of importance. Some African Countries that left significant footprints in the United States soil include, but are not limited to, Ghana, Sierra Leone, Nigeria, Somalia, Kenya, Eritrea, Ethiopia, Algeria, Egypt, Sudan, South Africa, Congo, and Liberia.

I believe that the Continent of Africa has 54 Countries and 4 Dependent Territories. Many borders were set by colonial occupiers with not much respect for racial bonds such as Tribal or family links, languages and so on.

More than a few people reject the word Black American for this reason. It seems to be a name that draws attention to skin color rather than a genuine National identification. That opinion is open to multiple opinions.

Watch this. As a stand-alone, in the mind of more people that you might imagine. Just saying African American points to a person's physical appearance. African American can be like an invisible ball and chain that affects everything, usually with unfavorable outcomes.

Simply assigning the word African American to a human has the power to imply a bankrupt North American citizenship. "You belong to another Country!" It is wicked racism. Psalm 71:4 KJV. "Deliver me, O my God, out of the hand of the wicked, out of the hand of the unrighteous and cruel man." It is time for a new season, a new beginning. Are you with us?

Slave holders introduced this thought to brainwash the slaves. "You should be thankful. Being a slave on my plantation has saved you from being a naked, ignorant **native**, living and dying in the unsafe African jungles."

Is capturing or buying people that already belong to God and exporting them for sell as slaves doing God a favor? Is it doing Black people a favor?

Once again, we are reminded of a viewpoint given through the scriptures.

Matthew 25:40 KJV "40 And the King shall answer and say unto them, Verily I say unto you, Inasmuch as ye have done it unto one of the least of these my brethren, ye have done it unto me."

You may have noticed a reference to the word "King." In the above scripture. Keep in mind this word, the Trinity. Said another way…the Father, the Son and the Holy Spirit.

While we have not succeeded at locating the actual word "trinity" in the bible. We can accept that trinity is derivative of the word "tri" which can translate to three and "unity" can translate to one. God is three distinct persons - the Father, the Son, and the Holy Spirit therefore a single unit.

God is the King of mankind. He rules as the trinity, mankind is his creation!

Matthew 26:41 KJV. "Watch and pray, that ye enter not into temptation: the spirit indeed is willing, but the flesh is weak." We should keep this truth in focus. Because of something that naturally exists in people, we are imperfect and there are times when the weak flesh will overcome the willing spirit.

When a person takes part in or ignores acts of prejudice towards people based on bodily features or racial grouping. When a person knows what is right but yields to temptation to satisfy a thirst for supremacy. That is a clear example of the weak flesh overpowering a willing spirit.

Reinforcing a point made earlier. We submit that the exact place on earth where God created the first man may not be known for good reasons. Perhaps God wanted to prevent any race from claiming supremacy in His name. Perhaps to prevent any Country from claiming supremacy in His name. He knew that the temptation would sometimes present challenges.

Attempts to normalize the word "African American" was put into motion without having any real consent from most of the people involved.

While African American is name used by large number of the public at large. Many Native Black Americans are not pleased. Endorsers appear to do nothing more than satisfy their own wants. Sometimes it seems their intent is only to nourish a hunger to please the powerful, the institution.

Seeds for African American name were planted during the pursuit of Civil Rights in the United States.

Luke 8:5-6-7-8 KJV, gives this wisdom. "A sower went out to sow his seed. Some fell upon a rock and as soon as it sprung up, it withered away, because it lacked moisture. Some fell among thorns and the thorns sprang up with it and choked it. Some fell on good ground, and sprang up, and bear fruit a hundredfold."

If you will, consider this comparison. We often hear the word…RACE. Sometimes it appears in a negative sense, sometime in a positive sense. As you know the term human describes all men, women, and children. The term human separates us from all other living life forms. Sadly, it seems that certain humans assumed the authority to plant a seed using the Bible as a good reason. Once planted, the African American seed sprang up…but thorns will choke it. It will wither away, because it lacks moisture.

It cannot bear good fruit because it has evil intent. The intent was to cause severe harm or downfall by depriving Black people born on United States soil…of their Constitutional rights. Said another way… of their citizenship.

We will tell you this. That seed is being choked by the thorns of uncertainty because the African American label can refer to more than one ethnic group. The name that was planted, African American shall wither away. A new seed, a new creation, Native Black American, has been planted on fruitful ground. We are thankful that by the grace of God it has started to take root. It will bear good fruit His will shall be done.

Again, hear ye these inspirational words from a very credible source, Exodus 3:14 King James version "I AM THAT I AM."

We submit that while it has not been commonly discussed. There have been attempts to avoid discussing the following fact.

Genesis 2:7 KJV "And the Lord God formed man of the dust of the ground." It is safe to believe that God had a purpose when He formed Native Black American men, women, and children from the dust of the United States.

But take a minute to consider this. It seems that a threat to the loss of supremacy can be powerful. So powerful that humans can be inspired to selectively control education and influence what is recorded as history.

Isaiah 5:2 KJV tells us this. "Woe unto them that call evil good, and good evil; that put darkness for light, and light for darkness; that put bitter for sweet, and sweet for bitter."

Native Black Americans did not create this difficult situation, but now we own it. Since we have found our correct racial identification, we must march forward in a way that serves God first, then the United States of America, and the best interest of all Native Black Americans.

We must abandon our feeling of calm satisfaction with or submission to reflections like "that is just the way it has always been."

We are not suggesting actions in the sense of violence. In fact, we strongly encourage a non-violent strategy to achieve recognition goals. Goals that include acceptance of a dignified racial name which promotes equality.

The intent is to motivate a new beginning, a new classification. A more productive future for Native Black Americans.

We should not… disrespect anybody belonging to any race classification within the human species.

Joshua 5:13 KJV tells us "And it came to pass, when Joshua was by Jericho, that he lifted up his eyes and looked, and, behold, there stood a man over against him with his sword drawn in his hand: and Joshua went unto him, and said unto him, Art thou for us, or for our adversaries?"

Perhaps said another way…are you with us, or against us?

Joshua 5:14 KJV. "And he said, Nay; but as captain of the host of the Lord am I now come. "

Could it be that the "captain of the host of the Lord" was the Son of God?

Could it be that captain of the host of the Lord? Was his sword drawn to reinforce that God was standing by to help those who help themselves.

Here we have an excellent standard giving Native Black Americans a goal to reach for. We have an obligation to press toward the mark for the prize of the higher calling, especially on behalf of our descendants. Stop bowing down the misleading race identification, African American. We must demonstrate that we have the courage to help ourselves by bringing about our own racial name…Native Black American!

Matthew 19:26 KJV tells us "But Jesus said unto them, with God all things are possible."

Chapter Three

The Winter Chapter

It you will pause for just a moment. Find a quiet place and mentally… rest peacefully. Break loose from the chains that hold back your imagination.

Early, early, early, one morning we found ourselves looking towards the rising sun. Our brainpower will keep us on track as to what is true or what is not. Even so, the mind's eye could easily reason that the sun began this day by rising from either the ground or the ocean.

That rising sun climbed slowly in the Eastern sky following what we believe to be a divinely guided path.

Ecclesiastes 3:1 KJV tells us "To everything there is a season, and a time to every purpose under the heaven."

Having fulfilled its assignments which included overcoming shadows of the night. The sun seemed to gradually sink down in the Western sky. Once again, the mind's eye reasoned that the sun just faded away, either into the ground or the ocean.

Imaging a huge, gold tinted moon…slowly appearing in the dark sky.

The moon can also project the reflection of a golden light across the ocean. That reflection could easily remind one of a gold tinted, hallway style runner carpet. It seemed to slowly unroll over a calm ocean.

See in your mind's eye, a golden footpath leading directly toward you. Think of a mysterious but tempting hand, making a gesture. It was urging you to take the first step. Listen to a hidden voice telling you to step out onto the water and follow the golden path. Matthew 14: 28 "And Peter answered him and said, Lord, if it be thou, bid me come unto thee on the water."

If you will, imagine a warm night and hearing ocean waves bumping against each other. The sounds are mentally pleasing…or relaxing.

But the calm of this quite night will be broken by evidence that a storm is coming. There is a sudden moist breeze that seems to wrap around you. Hear the soft, but scary sound of thunder in the empty…dark distance.

As the storm moved closer the wind became more intense.

The power of the wind creates a threating howl, it also gives the impression of having the ability to be destructive. As the sound of the wind comes closer it brushes noisily through the branches and leaves on nearby trees. Then, that unseen force moves on towards its unknown destination.

John 3:8 KJV tells us "The wind bloweth where it listeth, and thou hearest the sound thereof, but canst not tell whence it cometh, and whither it goeth."

Electric bolts of energy also referred to as lightning suddenly appeared to be tumbling aimlessly through the dark skies. The flashing lightning bolts had the brightness of a very hot fire, causing the dark skies to glow for a split second. That irregular and wobbling bright bolt of light briefly comes into sight, then quickly vanishes. One could easily sense that there could be an unearthly or supernatural connection.

A lighting flash is often followed by the muffled sound of rolling thunder echoing from the mist. The sound is generated by shock waves triggered when cool air collides with the lighting's intense heat. Those short-lived sounds start in a low tone but get louder. They remind one of the rhythms created by a drum roll

Remember Psalm 77:18 KJV? "The voice of thy thunder was in the heaven: the lightnings lightened the world: the earth trembled and shook." One could easily imagine hearing a voice from heaven.

Imagine that you can also hear the soothing tempo of dense rain falling on a tin roof. Rain gives the impression that each drop has its own soul or spiritual life especially when it seems to knock on the windowpanes. The wind and rain work together to produce a relaxing state of mind, often causing one to fall into a deep sleep.

While the original author/s could be identified as unknown, we can find the following quote in one of several manuscripts omitted from the Bible. They are often referred to as the non-canonical or lost biblical books.

The following quote is credited to Chapter 1, Verse 5, "Enoch's encounter with the two angels of God."

"And when I was asleep, great distress came up into my heart, and I was weeping with my eyes in sleep. I could not understand what this distress was, or what would happen to me. I eventually faded into a state of sleep and seemed to find myself awakened, but in the blurriness of a vision."

"A stairway appeared within the mist, and it reached all the way to the sky. Mysterious people were going up and going down on it."

Two angels have the privilege of being the only angels specifically named in Sacred scripture. They are Gabriel and Michael who were also holders of the title archangel. The title Archangel results when connecting two key words arch, and angel. The key word (arch) can be applied in several different ways. For the purposes of this writing 'arch' describes having authority over others within the same group. Archangel symbolically translates to "chief angel."

One of the critical duties assigned to Gabriel seems to be serving as an Archangel who comes bearing messages from God. On several occasions in the Bible, he is given the job of coming to earth to make important statement about a special event.

One of the critical duties assigned to Michael seems to be serving as a guardian. Michael is a warrior who defends of God's will. He stands strong with courage, moral strength, and justice. One of Michael's missions is to serve as a guardian especially for anyone willing to deny themself, take up their cross, and follow Jesus. Matthew 16:24 KJV.

Of interest, history is often the vision as recorded by the witness or an active participant in historical events. Sometimes the story is repeated hearsay provided by someone who was not directly involved. The recording of history is most often inspired by one or more of the following. Culture, economic status, level of education, geographical origin, the dominant race, religion, the primary holder of power and controller of real estate.

We continue to search for any biblical writing that that delivers absolute evidence giving either the racial group or the skin color of the archangels.

Remember that I described a vision. Remember that I saw this stairway which suddenly appeared within the mist. Its highest steps seemed to touch the clouds then fade away. Remember that a storm was approaching. Remember the display of lightning bolts and the sound of rolling thunder.

Remember, I reported that on the stairway there appeared a mysterious person. As I moved closer it became clear that the mysterious figure was encircled by a very bright light. I reported that it made a gesture with movements of fingers on the right hand. In that same moment the figure beckoned me by rotating his head from the left towards the right side. Suggesting that I should follow this mysterious person up the steps.

Looking back. Could the mysterious person have been the archangel, Gabriel?

Possibly he came to bring a message revealing a new creation. A new beginning. An unblemished racial identity for Black people who are home-grown, who are Natives, who are citizens of the United States American.

The specific place or location of a person's birth defines where that person is native to. For the purposes of this writing, the word native refers to people who were created from the clay or dust of The United States of America. We reject being branded as a new human group simply poured into an old name. Luke 5: 37 KJV tells us "And no man putteth new wine into old bottles; else the new wine will burst the bottles, and be spilled, and the bottles shall perish. 5: 38,"But new wine must be put into new bottles; and both are preserved."

Getting back to the dream…Standing in the lower court hallway and looking up one can count fifteen rising steps. I decided to take the first step and follow that mysterious figure. We climbed a simi-circular stairway. Occasionally passing through fog, it seemed like a journey that would never end. With the passing time we finally reached the upper court.

At the top of the stairway, unknown forces caused me to briefly pause. I was facing a massive Medieval era castle door. I estimated that the door measure twelve feet high and it was constructed from what appeared to be solid oak. The massive doors were held in place by oversized iron hinges and the old-fashioned door lock handle was made of gold.

Simply standing in front of that door caused a level of fear. Why was I experiencing the emotion called fear, why not lean on my faith?

Joshua 1:9 KJV "Have not I commanded thee? Be strong and of a good courage; be not afraid, neither be thou dismayed: for the Lord thy God is with thee whithersoever thou goest." So, my eyes closed for a moment of reflection then…I pushed aside that fear which stood in my path. I took a deep breath, called upon my strength of will and pulled the door open.

Psalm 138:7 KJV. "Though I walk in the midst of trouble, thou wilt revive me: thou shalt stretch forth thine hand against the wrath of mine enemies, and thy right hand shall save me." I prayed, asking God to stretch forth his hand against any possible wrath. Then I walked through the open door.

The passageway was dimly lit by a series of burning torches that were set high on the walls. The flickering torch flames caused shadows that created moving images on the walls. Those images seemed to be alive.

This certainly was a time when my faith was put to the test.

I found myself in a room which did not have a traditional square or rectangular layout. It was a round or circle design. Circles have no edges or corners. Circles symbolize seamless and continuing harmony… where the circle begins, is where that same circle ends. The eternal trait of a circle reminds one of the eternal traits linking "as far as the east is from the west."

It was later revealed that this would be only the first in a series of 7 round or circle shaped rooms. In the center of each of the 7 rooms, there will be another door…leading to another circled room.

The first room was very dim. I could see the flames on the tops of flickering torches, they sent out a golden glow. Without seeing any human body, I felt a push on the shoulder and walked forward.

While you know what the reality is. Allow yourself to imagine watching the rising sun overtake the darkness. The rising sun appears to emerge from the ground or the oceans. Perhaps from the mountains or man-made structures. As a comparison look back, remember when the flickering flames overcame the darkness.

I counted twelve steps as I walked forward. Suddenly a voice that had alarming, thunder-like qualities echoed from the dim emptiness. The tone of the voice gave the impression of having no respect for humanity. It had indicators of evil intent. Lacking any hint of mercy, that voice shouted the word slave. I supposed that the word "slave" was intended to condemn my soul. To force me to my knees. But…It only gave strength to my will power.

Previously, I had mentioned that the flickering torches seemed to produce moving images on the walls. In this setting there was this feeling of being surrounded by people. I thought that I could hear moans voicing agony.

Could those moans have been from the spirits of people who were forced to surrender their freedom to Trading Companies. People who had been motivated by the threat of looking into the business end of pistols and long barrel guns. Life or death situations can force surrender against your will.

Trading Companies were organizations conducting several goods for profit businesses that often operated in overseas territories. One of the Trading Companies' principal business models included human trafficking. They purchased or captured African people who were quickly classified as nothing more than property. The same people were bound by chains and warehoused in the cargo holds of sailing ships. Afterwards they were transported to distant lands and sold as chattel or personal property.

The Old and New Testaments have scriptures that speak of slavery. While slavery was an accepted part of life among many nations especially during the Biblical age. We find no evidence that slavery was God driven. We can find these words in Exodus 21:16. "And he that stealeth a man, and selleth him, or if he be found in his hand, he shall surely be put to death."

Upon entering the second room, once again I found it very difficult to see. Just as previously mentioned there were flickering torches that had a hypnotic pull. Think of a lighthouse beam guiding ships on a stormy night.

I heard yet another menacing voice. It projected thunder-like qualities as it echoed from the emptiness. The tone of a threating voice called out the word Negro with the clear goal of hinting that simply by name. Negroes were judged inferior. Proverbs 17:20 KJV, "He who has a crooked mind finds no good. And he who is perverted in his language falls into evil."

The name Negro has many roots. Tracing one of those roots will lead to the early 1400s. History suggest that one set of footprints will lead to people located in Africa along the Niger River. At one time Africa was referred to as the Dark Continent. Dark Continent could lead the mind's eye to see a land that has many problems. Dark Continent suggests that the entire Negro race is afflicted with being timid, lazy, lacking in the ability to think. Perhaps the intent was to suggest that Negroes were just born inferior.

In the third room, there were also distant flickering torches that produced a golden brilliance around the room. As in the past, flames from the torches caused me to see shadows moving on the walls as if they were living bodies.

I heard yet another menacing voice thundering from the emptiness. Once more, without any hint of compassion it called out yet another insulting racial identity. Nigger! Perhaps earlier but give or take, the roots of that term can be traced to or around the 1600s.

The word, Nigger has many purposes. As a rule, it is used to put a label on people of color. The main goal is to imply that when calling someone a Nigger you are judging the target as slow-moving and timid. A person that will steal rather than earn. For so-called supremist, Niggers are seen as Buffoons. Ignorant people whose level of intelligence is often judged by stupid behavior which caused laughing at the Nigger…not with them.

Food for thought. Matthew 7:1-2 KJV "Judge not, that ye be not judged. For with what judgment ye judge, ye shall be judged: and with what measure ye mete, it shall be measured to you again."

The Biblical ruling "Judge not, that ye be not judged" is often ignored. Sadly, at times some religious leaders fail to meet biblical judging values.

In the fourth room, one more time I saw flickering golden torches but now the glow seemed weaker. It looks as if the night shadows were slowly being overcome by hints of the dawn awakening. This signals the creation of another day, a new beginning.

I heard yet another menacing voice thundering from the emptiness. It seemed a thorny effort to condemn and discourage. Once again without any hint of compassion it called out yet another insulting racial identity, Colored.

Colored was created to replace the words Negro and Nigger. It was intended to serve as a more polite labelling of Native Black Americans who had suffered generations of discrimination. Colored is a dog whistle word.

White is much paler than other colors. All the same time White is a color. All colors have varying shades of tint. People of color is a term open to much debate because all races could be described as Colored people.

The original source of the [Colored] remains mysterious. The institution skillfully and often by corrupt means, made sure that those previously identified as Negro, Nigger now Colored stayed in their place. One source of power was Jim Crow laws. When interpreted Jim Crow means "Negro laws".

In the fifth room, flickering torches continued to be visible. However, the images of dark shadows dancing on the walls were more difficult to see. One could say that the threating shadows were being overcome by a powerful light gifted from a divine source.

Imagine lifting your eyes towards the Eastern skyline. The night hours bring darkness. But…early, early in the morning, see God's creation which begins as a trace of light coming into view as a half circle. Watch while that light slowly expands toward the outer edge of the half circle. In time, unless there is a storm, the entire sky takes on a soothing blue color.

I heard another menacing voice thundering from the emptiness. Once again, without any hint of compassion the voice called out the words Afro American, just another way of saying non-citizen Black American.

Afro American was a name popular for a brief stretch in the 1950s and 1960s. Footprints leading to the term can be traced to about 1853, perhaps further back. We believe that Afro American was favored by many Black American people who were searching for a dignified racial classification. It is difficult to pin a specific birthday for Afro American. The term balances on a slope more slippery than the current made-up name…African American.

I was troubled because it seems that the use of racial names like Afro and African American were intended to stand in the way of Black people born in the United States. The trick is…attach a Foreign Country name suggesting that Black people born in America are really citizens of some other Country.

Citizenship can be defined as membership and owed allegiance to a Country in which a person has been born or they have complied with naturalization legal requirements. Citizens have well-defined required duties, and responsibilities. Among citizenship benefits are certain rights, privileges, and protection.

One conclusion could be…to any Black person born in the United States who choose to identify as African American. You are placing a ball and chain on the future of all Black people born in the United States of America.

Accepting the title African American equates to falling to your knees and surrendering your race to ethnic cleansing perhaps…ethnic lynching .

In the sixth room from the dim emptiness, I heard another menacing voice thundering "Black People". It also called out without any hint of compassion. I was concerned because for some people when they use the word "Black People" it has an underlying discriminating intent. Remember dog whistles? Can it be just another not very well-hidden attempt to downgrade the birthright of United States of America citizenship.

Using of the word Black people to replace the word American people is like swinging a sword that has two edges. The blade can cut from either side. It is necessary to call attention to this fact. Prior to the 1960's, identifying any Black person as a Black this or Black that…was considered insulting. However, the attitude of Black people changed. God works in mysterious ways. We are who we are…it is now an honor to be called a Black person.

There have been ongoing awakening experiences for Black people who were sold as slaves in many different Countries. We are talking mainly about Countries which have beaches which touch waters from the Atlantic Ocean (Western side) or the Caribbean Sea.

Events during the North American Civil War, World War One and World War Two awakened many who had slipped into an attitude of accepting slavery. Examples of awakening include these facts. Black men and women were able to earn leadership ranks. They proved that

Blacks could accomplish missions which required brain power and courage. Black men discovered that foreign military leadership valued and used their war fighting skills. Such recognition was shallow in the United States.

Galatians 5:1 KJV tells us to "Stand fast therefore in the liberty wherewith Christ hath made us free and be not entangled again with the yoke of bondage." You are who you are, stand up and reach for the higher calling. Returning home to humbly accept Jim Crow laws is no longer acceptable.

Without argument the experiences during the wars gave Black people a strong reason. Military members returning from fighting battles on foreign soil were awakened to reasons to seek dignity on United States of America soil.

Words that amount to any type of racial judging and the denial of earned opportunities simply because of one's skin color are evil. We are reminded of Psalm 94:4 KJV "How long shall they utter and speak hard things?"

Another answer can be found in an example of wisdom. Matthew 26:41 KJV "Watch and pray: the spirit indeed is willing, but the flesh is weak." Three major weak points of the flesh for this writing are… the power of entitlement…the benefit of having the upper hand based on skin color…and presumed supremacy, which ironically can be empowered by those who surrender to it.

In the seventh room, I heard yet another voice. Still coming from an unseen source, the distinctive thundering tone continued. However, there seemed to be a different spirit. I heard a voice that reassured me it uplifted my faith.

This time I was touched with happiness because the roaring voice was no longer threatening. This time the voice had an inspiring tone. I decided to lift my head in defiance and step forward. Philippians 3:14 KJV "press toward the mark for the prize of the high calling of God in Christ Jesus."

Light from the torches began to fade. As time passed natural light began to take over which made brighter the path.

Looking once again into the Eastern sky. I noticed that dawn had begun to usher in a new day. An impressive sunrise was starting the process of showering the earth with a warm, but intense glow.

Daniel 5:5 KJV "In the same hour came forth fingers of a man's hand, and wrote over against the candlestick upon the plaister of the wall of the king's palace: and the king saw the part of the hand that wrote."

If you will, imagine seeing a wall and this mysterious hand suddenly coming into view, writing on a wall. Imagine seeing a new racial classification written out. At last, a race classification of our choice. One that allows those who may find the courage…to demand recognition of this new racial identity that is without blemish. That name is… Native Black American.

A racial identity that is true. A privilege earned by birthright, by sacrificing life and limb as members of the Armed Forces, by helping to build the United States of America making our Country a desired destination. By waiting on the Lord. Psalm 27:14 KJV "Wait on the Lord: be of good courage, and he shall strengthen thine heart: wait, I say, on the Lord."

The painfully slow but deliberate progress of Native black Americans for 5 plus generations. More likely than not, was part of His plan when God created the heaven and the earth.

Jeremiah 1:5 KJV tells us words to this effect. "Before I formed thee in the belly I knew thee; and before thou camest forth out of the womb I sanctified thee."

Additionally, Revelation 3:8 KJV provides this reassurance. "I know thy works: behold, I have set before thee an open door, and no man can shut it: for thou hast a little strength, and hast kept my word, and hast not denied my name." God will shut some doors and when it is His will, other doors shall open.

There is no doubt that God opened the door of no return which led to His creating a new race. Once opened, Africans who were controlled by force passed through that door. They were loaded in the storage space of sailing ships and set sail on the ocean. Their journey ended at the shores of the land of promise. The United States of America! Proverbs 3:5-6 KJV. "Trust in the Lord with all thine heart; and lean not unto thine own understanding. In all thy ways acknowledge him, and he shall direct thy paths."

If you believe. Psalm 119:133 KJV offers this promising choice "Order my steps in thy word: and let not any iniquity have dominion over me."

Stay on guard. There will be expected and unexpected events that you will be either unwilling to accept or unable to understand. From time to time, God will close doors that you want to be open. If your ego and courage will allow it. If you honestly look back on footprints left on the trail during your life journey. You will find that a closed door led to a beneficial door opening.

Often, that closed door helps to strengthen us and encourages us to reach for a higher calling. Said another way…find a different path to follow.

We now believe that a door of opportunity has opened. We must take this opening to rise from our bent knees. Going forward we should reject any racial identification given by the institution or some other racial group.

We also expect to hear this question. How did this new racial identity, Native Black American identity evolve? Watch this.

Native. A person born in a specified place or associated with a place by birth. There is a thin line between Native and Indigenous.

Indigenous. One definition tells us that indigenous applies when a person is created or naturally exists in a place or Country rather than arriving from another location.

Ethnicity or Race. There is also a thin line between the definition of ethnicity and race. Definitions which can be influenced by several factors.

Basically, ethnicity is a social label. Those labels tend to be classified by language or dialect, behaviors, food, clothing, hair, shared moral values, certain aspects of religion, and a cultural, heritage connection. Ethnicity can also be influenced by where one is born and the surroundings or conditions in which one lives.

Race or human grouping generally refers to a person's skin color, eye shapes and pupil colors as well as certain facial features. Hair texture for example curly, wavy, or straight and its color. A person's physical looks are influenced by several factors. Some factors are genetic structure codes and climatic conditions where his or her ancestors developed.

For about 5 generations, Native Black Americans have been able to trace their lineage from common ancestors. However, during slavery tracing was discouraged you could say that it was blocked. Keeping a record of family lineage could bring trouble for African slaves.

There is no disputing that some individual physical looks associated with Native Black Americans are traceable to the Continent of Africa. However, a solution to all issues involving the name African American cannot be found by solely leaning on physical looks linked to Africa.

The truth regarding our racial physical looks involves incidents that cannot be ignored. For just about 5 generations in the Native Black American world. There has been an untold number of male and female mixing encounters that crossed over several racial bridges.

Looking back, we find evidence of not agreed to intimate relations between Black North Americans and persons of other races. On the other hand, we can find evidence of agreed to intimate relations involving the same people. Remember that scripture that talks about, "the spirit indeed is willing, but the flesh is weak." We submit that the blood or genes flowing through the veins of a high percent of Black people born in the United States of America. It is eternally integrated with the blood or genetics of people from several different racial groups. The result is a new creation....a new race.

There are some Native Black Americans who may not know about or for various reasons choose to deny that they have blood or genetics from other than African sources. Consider this wisdom from Malachi

2:10 KJV. "Have we not all one father? hath not one God created us?"

Genesis 2:7 KJV "And the Lord God formed man of the dust of the ground and breathed into his nostrils the breath of life; and man became a living soul."

This already said. We believe that God formed Native Black Americans from the United States of America dust or clay. He breathed life into them, and He created a new living soul. That act of God and the 14th Amendment to the U.S. Constitution gave citizenship to Black people born in the United States. The two breathed life into a new name... Native Black American.

Often one can hear the following words during funeral ceremonies when it is time to commit the deceased to the ground or before remains are handed over for cremation. "Dust you came from, to dust you will return." Could the following words of wisdom have influence those thoughts.

Genesis 3:19 KJV "till thou return unto the ground; for out of it wast thou taken: for dust thou art, and unto dust shalt thou return."

For the majority of Native Black Americans. We present this as matter for thought...when we die our body shall return to the dust from whence, it was taken. As a figure of speech...taken from the dust of the United States.

When we die. People often set aside separate cemeteries or final resting places for our earthly bodies. We are talking about segregated burial grounds. We ask these questions...are our spirits segregated in heaven or hell? Are Jim Crow laws enforced in heaven or hell? The Holy word presents a clue.

Job 34:15 KJV "All flesh shall perish together, and man shall turn again unto dust." Ecclesiastes 3:20 KJV. All go unto one place; all are of the dust, and all turn to dust again. No mention of racial segregation.

This subject has already been talked about. After a person dies, and when the time for resurrection is upon us. When the book of life is opened, and judgement is made. Will our spiritual body keep the same race in heaven?

If you will…hear 1Corinthians15:35 KJV. "But some man will say, How are the dead raised up, and with what body do they come?"

1 Corinthians15:38 KJV gives this answer. "God giveth it a body as it hath pleased him."

As previously stated, Native Black Americans are the only racial group on earth that has been either assigned or just accepted a different racial naming about every 53 years. Why do we accept the constant changes? What is the value added?

Many Native Black Americans are sick and tired of repeatedly changing the National racial flag that we march under. Tell those somebodies, cease fire.

We do not know about you, but we believe that God is not looking over his shoulder watching the constant changing. However, if we continue to just accept the changes perhaps, we should look over our own shoulders.

By the grace of God… we are…who…we are.

What is Culture? Culture is generally accepted standards found in States, Counties, municipalities, organizations, social groups, foundations, and so on. Some examples of culture can involve similarities shared by more than one person. It could include traditional beliefs, clothing, the source and level of education, material values, fraternal and sorority affiliations, groups sharing the same religion, family values and other standards not spoken.

At the risk of facing resistance, we submit that Native Black Americans have absorbed the culture of many different societies. However, let history show that now we have developed our own Native Black American culture.

Power can lead to corruption. Sometimes, people in power will be tempted and try to distort the truth by selecting certain history to skip over. They arrange the story line with a narrative which may inspire opinions. One goal is to justify claims of superior intelligence and dominance over others.

James 1:14 KJV "14 But every man is tempted, when he is drawn away of his own lust, and enticed." The act of slavery in the United States was in part, driven by the lust for wealth that required the benefits afforded by free human labor. Some use verses in the scriptures to justify slavery.

In this writing we are moved to emphasize that during the past five (5) plus generations. Native Black Americans were not brought from another Country. We are an act of God…we are Native…we are Indigenous…we are constitutional citizens of the United States of America.

With that said…let us return to discussing experiences in the 7th room.

1 John 2:8 KJV "the darkness is past. The true light now shineth."

Matthew 7:14 KJV "Because strait is the gate, and narrow is the way, which leadeth unto life, and few there be that find it." Have you ever heard anybody suggest that the right path to follow is one that is straight and narrow?

Another scripture tells us this. Matthew 7:13 KJV "For wide is the gate, and broad is the way, that leadeth to destruction."

The wide door (gate) in that scripture could talk to, while the spirit is willing, the flesh is weak. Sometimes temptation can lead to decisions that are influenced by the reward of winning. Greed can make things cloudy when one must separate the right from the wrong. The wrong decision could lead to the eventual loss of your moral dignity. Others may not know, but you will.

Upon entering the 7th room. I saw a human-like figure that stood surrounded by a cloud which had a certain glow. I fell to my knees in terror and tried to cover my eyes.

Suddenly, I heard a deep-tone voice that had echoing qualities. It had a calming touch. I heard these words. Do not be weighed down by fear.

This could have been the archangel, Michael.

One of the critical duties assigned to Michael seems to be serving as a guardian Archangel. Michael is a warrior who defends of God's will. He stands strong with courage, moral strength, and justice.

Michael performs the duties as one of the defenders, foremost for anyone who is willing to take up the cross of Jesus and follow him.

Matthew 16:24 KJV "Then said Jesus unto his disciples, If any man will come after me, let him deny himself, and take up his cross, and follow me."

The act of offering or allowing yourself to suffer while taking up the burden carried by another person reminds us of spoken or written reports from history. We are talking about the life of a man named, Simon of Cyrene.

Cyrene should not be interpreted as Simon's last name. Instead, please note that Cyrene refers to the homeland that Simon came from.

Sometimes unspoken codes exist. It seems that human culture or the rules of society use a person's skin color, race, and place of birth to define where another person should fit in the ruling social structure.

Oh yes, let us not overlook speech accents or the way words are pronounced. Accents can define a person…sometimes the result is favorable other times, not.

Normally human society sets up a defined pecking order driven in part by one or more of those above-mentioned factors.

The Simon that we refer to had traveled from Cyrene, an ancient Greek city that fell under Roman rule. The city is within the territory now called Libya, located on the northern African continent.

Reasonably speaking, because of Africa's extremely hot climate. People who are Native to the Continent of Africa generally have a range of skin colors. Colors that are darker than skin shades found in cold climates.

Perhaps the exceptionally hot climate is what caused some history writers to suppose that Simon had either a dark or olive skin shade. A Black man.

Others history writers have different opinions or expressions of doubt regarding Simon's racial group. Could those opinions have hidden desires or agendas that talk to racial supremacy? Interesting!

The KJV or King James Version of the Holy Bible specifically shares with us these words "A man of Cyrene, Simon." We believe it is by intent that omitting the color of Simon's skin is not an issue for God.

2 Peter 1:20 KJV tells us "Knowing this first, that no prophecy of the scripture is of any private interpretation."

Some believe that Simon of Cyrene was in Jerusalem for reasons connected to the ritual of Passover.

Matthew 27:24 KJV. "Following the closing of the trial of Jesus. "When Pilate saw that he could prevail nothing, he took water, and washed his hands before the multitude, saying, I am innocent of the blood of this just person." .

Matthew 27:26 KJV. "Then released he Barabbas unto them: and he delivered Jesus to be crucified."

Matthew 27:32 KJV. "And as they came out, they found a man of **Cyrene**, Simon by name: they compelled Simon to bear the cross."

Mark 15:21 KJV. "And they compel one Simon a Cyrenian, who passed by, coming out of the country, the father of Alexander and Rufus, to bear his cross."

Luke 23:26 KJV. "And as they led him away, they laid hold upon one Simon, a Cyrenian, coming out of the country, and on him they laid the cross, that he might bear it after Jesus."

John 19:17 KJV. And he bearing his cross went forth into a place called the place of a skull, which is called in the Hebrew Golgotha."

In the context of this writing use of the word bear is intended to mean…to carry the weight of something from one place to another. It can also point to accepting and bearing hardships for someone.

The scriptures give evidence that Simon Cyrene did give physical relief to Jesus by carrying the cross.

However, Jesus was also bearing that cross, but from a mental point of view. Jesus humbled himself and became obedient to scriptural prophecy. He voluntary suffered a brutal death on the cross.

Matthew26:39 KJV. "And he went a little farther, and fell on his face, and prayed, saying, O my Father, if it be possible, let this cup pass from me: nevertheless not as I will, but as thou wilt."

The assignment given to Simon Cyrene may have appeared to be a random selection. While he was identified by the ruling society to carry the cross for Jesus, the mission was decided in advance by the divine one. Simon Cyrene was fulfilling God's pre-ordained will.

Surely that task must have given Simon a difficult burden. With confidence we believe that even if it lingered for only a moment. Carrying the heavy wooden cross tempted Simon to disobey authority.

1 Corinthians 10:13 KJV "But God is faithful, who will not suffer you to be tempted above that ye are able; but will with the temptation also make a way to escape, that ye may be able to bear it."

Pause for a moment. Remember that the guardian angel Michael performs the duties of a defender, mainly for anyone who is willing to take up the cross of Jesus and follow him.

Luke 9:23 KJV "And he said to them all, if any man will come after me, let him deny himself, and take up his cross daily, and follow me."

We can hear readers whispering, how does Simon of Cyrene impact on this writing?

We should consider that Simon sacrificed himself to bear the burden of another human. A person whom he was aware of but did not personally know. Simon stepped forward to assist a person who suffered prejudice, a person who was considered not good enough and rejected by many. Perhaps Simon Cyrene felt that he had a debt to pay.

We believe that Simon Cyrene set a worthy example for Native Black Americans to follow. Galatians 6:2 KJV. "Bear ye one another's burdens, and so fulfil the law of Christ."

In my mind I can imagine the guardian Archangel Michael asking, how long…how long…how much longer will it take for Native Black Americans open their eyes that they may see?

Stop explaining your suffering by giving power to that mysterious idol called "The Man." For example. If it were not…for the Man stopping me, I could have gotten that promotion. Did you prepare yourself, were you the most qualified?

Stop accepting or settling for second, third or any lesser class…in any society. Stop tolerating the empty African American racial title. It is just one more…nobody…racial title, an attack our dignity.

Stop eating crumbs that fall from the King's table. Prepare yourself. Get a high-quality education. Practice and demand high moral standards. Work to become an employer rather than living life as an employee. Help other Native Black Americans earn a "win."

Think of and copy the humble support given by Simon Cyrene when he carried the cross for Jesus. Under no circumstance should you fail to voluntarily help another Native Black American to carry their cross. Especially when much effort and personal sacrifice is required by you.

Galatians 6:2 KJV "Bear ye one another's burdens, and so fulfil the law of Christ."

The voice called out with a hint of joy…Native Black American. Put the cross on your shoulder and follow the path laid out for you. Lead your race forward.

Stand strong with noble courage. Make known with pride I Am who I Am. Native Black American.

CHAPTER FOUR
The Spring Chapter

Exodus 14:15-16 KJV "And the Lord said unto Moses, Wherefore criest you thou unto me: Lift thou up thy rod, and stretch out thine hand over the sea, and divide it." God has said "He will not fail thee, neither forsake thee: fear not, neither be dismayed." Call on him while he is near. Call on your courage. Stand up, give your support to taking this new racial name.

2 Corinthians 5:17 KJV, "Therefore if any man be in Christ, he is a new creature: old things are passed away; behold, all things are become new. "

Native Black Americans are a new creation having fought for and earned deliverance from slavery. On the surface, we have overcome the insulting Jim Crow version of the ten Commandments.

After going through the Narrow door (gate). Despite walking on slippery stones while facing racism barriers based mostly on assumed supremacy. We cannot surrender to the Jim Crow Ten Commandments that were enforced yesterday. Native Black Americans, arise, stand with courage. Your time has come. God has lit a candle or torch which will illuminate our path forward.

Pause for a moment…listen to a gentle voice moving about on a warm breeze. Can you hear that voice whispering, "why would God allow anyone that He loved to experience the pain of slavery?" That comment is not just talking about Black slaves. Some form of slavery has affected all races since the dawn of an organized society. Isaiah 55:8-9 KJV tells us "For my thoughts are not your thoughts, neither are your ways my ways, saith the Lord; For as the heavens are higher than the earth, so are my ways higher than your ways, and my thoughts than your thoughts."

Once again…remember this. The biblical number eight represents a new beginning, A new order or creation. Eight declares a promising future.

Do not let any person who is not obeying accepted rules of a civilized and moral society hold back your new beginning, your new racial order. The number 8 announces a new creation and that is Native Black American!

There are many different religious denominations. There are also several different bibles including newer versions of the older bibles that in general only repeat established scriptures using different words.

In this 7th room, if there is a listening ear, one could hear a thundering voice declaring that we have not been given, but we have now earned our freedom. We have broken the slavery chains and shackles. We have faith in our Lord and savior. We have gained from the benefit of education.

For 5 plus generation we have walked through 7 different names that we accepted to identify our race. Although events must have been according to God's will, He has now exhibited favor to Native Black Americans. God has armed us with wisdom, courage and the will to win. Matthew 5:16 KJV. "Let your light so shine before men, that they may see your good works, and glorify your Father which is in heaven."

The season and time have come when we must demonstrate the essential level of self-respect and courage to take on a new name that is principled and has credibility. A National racial identity that we are willing to fight for.

We thank God because we believe that at last, he has set aside a race name or identification that has its own independent origin. An identity without blemish and not named by the institution or some other racial group.

This is the first step on a defining journey. This journey cannot end as a failure, that is not an option! This is also a most worthy reason to celebrate.

A percussion instrument is a musical instrument that vibrates in response to various influences such as being struck by an object. Moving special parts of a musical instrument can also influence the making of sounds. The material used to build the instrument set the tone and amplify the sound.

For centuries, one special percussion instrument called the bell has been used to make sounds that can be heard over long distances. Sounds from a bell announce major events and remember this. People are influenced by messages associated with a variety of sounds given off by a bell.

As a stand-alone, the physical image of a bell...even a photo or painting of a bell can prompt a person to pause for a moment and give respect. The bell seems to have certain mysterious, hypnotic-like qualities.

One of the most important symbols that talk to the proud heritage of the respected and admired United States of America is the Liberty Bell.

Leviticus 25:10 KJV includes these words. "Proclaim liberty throughout all the land unto all the inhabitants thereof." That quote can be seen engraved on the Liberty Bell in Philadelphia, Pennsylvania. The Liberty Bell was at first labeled as the State House Bell. During the 1800's as the United States continued to break free from the chains of Colonization. The bell became known as the Liberty Bell.

Citizens who advocated a total abolition of slavery "throughout all the land unto all the inhabitants" of the United Sates. Adopted the Liberty Bell image and its sounds as symbols of hope.

Native Black Americans, a people whose creation was sealed by God, have been starved by so-called equal but separate laws. With will power the same humans have kept in mind the Biblical story of Jacob's Ladder. For that ladder points to a connection between heaven and earth.

Equal but separate laws are interesting, it is a creative use of words.

People who assume supremacy believe that they have the sole right to determine what is evenly balanced. They have creative views when "Proclaiming liberty throughout all the land unto all the inhabitants thereof."

Just because a person does not have a physical appearance like yours, this does not necessarily mean that they are your enemy.

However, just because a person does have a physical appearance like yours, this does not necessarily mean that they are your friend.

Always govern yourself fortified with the truth. If any doubt should arise, ask this Joshua 5:13 KJV question. "Are you for us or for our enemies?"

Isaiah 2:3 KJV "And many people shall go and say, Come ye, and let us go up to the mountain of the Lord." There is no mountain too difficult to climb, too far to march around especially when the mark for the prize of the higher calling includes the promise of a dignified race name.

To anyone reading this writing please do not think over any notion that we are urging, nor will we participate in any attempt to commit treason against any United States of American Federal, State, or municipal Governments.

The truth is Black people added strength and value to the struggle that led to the Declaration of Independence by the Unted States of America.

And…despite the institution relentlessly counting Black people as slaves, semi-free Americans, and second-class citizens. Black men and women voluntarily suffered injury, many even made the ultimate sacrifice with their life to pay their portion of the cost for their Country's freedom. Deliberate sacrifices made that were beneficial to some citizens who did not…who will not value efforts by Black people. But…their outlook really does not matter.

John 15:13. KJV "Greater love hath no man than this, that a man lay down his life for his friends."

Think of an hourglass, some may use the term sand timer. The purpose of that device is measuring the passing of time. Its structure involves two glass bulbs connected by a narrow opening which controls the rate of sand flowing from the upper bulb to the lower one. Time is measured by finding how long it takes for the flow of sand from the upper glass bulb to fall into the lower bulb. Time and events equal… history.

History tells us about architectural influences coming from Native Black Americans which helped to build some of America's most important buildings. Perhaps some consider it a valid moral balance if they with intent omit records. If we let anyone succeed in bending what is true history about Native Black American contributions. We help to erase awareness of our valuable history. Time and events evenly balance…history.

Think of engineering skills displayed by slaves and free Black people who were paid the lowest wage, if any. Buildings and monuments that they helped to erect still stand as sentinels to freedom today. Some prominent examples include the United States Capitol and White House structures.

Scottish masons trained enslaved and free Black people at construction sites and the government's stone quarry located in Aquia, Virginia. They blasted, cut, and broke rough stone from an open face mine.

The masonic brotherhood may have set aside a selected few, guiding them to look towards the rising sun for a new beginning, a new direction to travel.

Both free and slave craftsmen worked jointly with skilled stonemasons and other organizations to produce or create. That process often-included Stone masons who were immigrants mainly from Germany, England, Ireland, Scotland, Italy, Greece and Egypt.

How long…how long will some assume the sole right to travel on the currents of the winds vainly attempting to redirect, erase or modify history? Ignoring events, banning books, destroying statues will not change history.

Over and over, this point has been previously stated. The blood or hereditary flowing through the veins of a high percent of Black people born in the United States, is eternally integrated with the blood or hereditary of people from more than one racial group. Again, the uniqueness of our evolution cast a shadow on the truth when trying to use African American to identify Black people born in the United States.

We should be determined in our journey for racial identity freedom to connect with the past and unite with the future. It is our responsibility. Why not look at the success of other cultures observing how they capture their own history. Why not apply more self-responsibility to preserving our own history. Why not step forward and say no...we will pursue our mission to stand erect and say I am who I am.

We remember one Lewis Latimer, born to slave parents who had gained their freedom. Beginning at the age 15 Latimer served as a sailor with the U.S. Navy during the American Civil war.

After his service to his Country Latimer developed his knowledge of engineering concepts and his skills involving the creation of technical pictures or drawings.

Thomas Edison invented the light bulb. However, it was Latimer who found a way to create a carbon filament for use within the lightbulb. The carbon filament had a longer life span than paper-based filaments. That engineering contribution extended the life of the lightbulb and helped the success of Edison's invention. Latimer was a valued member and the lone Black American on Edison's elite staff. Latimer also worked with Alexander Graham Bell Inventions.

We are reminded of another brave citizen-soldier whose parents were a Black American man and American Indian woman.

That was Crispus Attucks who is believed to be the first man to die while participating in action that would lead to the American Revolutionary War in March 1770. He paid the ultimate sacrifice during a scrimmage with the British Army which occupied Boston.

Crispus Attucks began life as a slave in Boston. He escaped the oppression of bondage by voluntarily serving as a seaman sailing on Boston based ships for nearly 20 years. While the salary earned was less than what was paid to White seamen working at the same jobs. He did earn a salary.

Crispus Attucks lived under the power of legal segregation, discrimination, and shady judicial equality. All just because of his race and skin color. Those thorns in his flesh did not stop Crispus Attucks from voluntarily stepping forward when the call to defend the United Stated touched him.

Crispus Attucks sacrificed his life while helping to make America a great Nation as God planned. His sacrifice was act of noble-minded behavior on behalf of his Country. The same Country that walk all over the dignity of Crispus Attucks.

John 15:13 KJV tells us "Greater love hath no man than this, that a man lay down his life for his friends." Please keep in mind that the scripture quoted does not set aside or separate man by race or skin color. It simply specified "that a man lay down his life for his friends."

If you will, travel with us as we continue to tear open the curtain used by the recorders of history to hide or weaken the contributions made by many Native Black Americans.

We are talking about loyal people who worked for, fought for, and died for their commitment to helping with the formation of a free Nation. A self-governing Republic. Republic is a term from the Latin language. The word describes political power held by the people through their elected or appointed representatives. Not simply power held by a single person.

Come with us, hear this appeal to give justified attention to yet another Native Black American who suffered lifelong denial of his individual freedom. Despite that, he stood strong to help secure freedom of the United States of America.

Allow the eye of your mind to place you at the intersection of High Street and Delaware Avenue in Burlington, New Jersey.

You may know that at the end of High Street there is a large metal anchor displayed as a monument to those who sailed the Delaware River and other large bodies of water. Anchors are used to secure or stabilize a ship to minimize drifting of the vessel. Native Black Americans are by law and facts anchored in the United States soil. We cannot lay down our arms or betray our reason for creation and drift to the right or to the left of the will of God.

Think of a large Schooner class sailing boat. It has two tall and one smaller ships' mast or poles. The two high poles hold large canvas sails used mainly for power. The smaller pole holds a sail that helps with power and steering. Allow your mind's eye to imagine watching as the wind is slowly pushing the boat on the Delaware river towards the Port of Burlington NJ.

After dockworkers tied the ship to the dock think of watching the spirit of one Black man walking down a ramp used as a footway between the ship and dock. He is holding a rifle in his right hand and has a canvas sea bag thrown over his left shoulder.

During the American Revolution he served with the 2nd New Jersey Regiment seeing combat at Trenton, Princeton, and Monmouth, New Jersey.

This Black American patriot was a battlefield drummer who soldiered physically close to General George Washington, who would be elected as the first President of the United States. The unidentified soldier-drummer had the unique honor of having his Honorable Discharge from the Continental Army signed by General Washington.

We submit that one will find clear associations of time and distance factors when reviewing one Biblical chapter of historical events. Psalm 103:12 KJV uses these words as a measurement. "As far as the East is from the West."

We point out this similarity. "As far as the East is from the West" can talk to the staying power of ancient drums. The study of drums used for military purposes reveals a long presence in history which could lead one to believe that battle drums have been around forever.

The battlefield drummer would give different drumbeats to send the orders from a leader controlling the battlefield tactics. The drumbeats were also used to control mass movement and other actions by military units with discipline and order. It seems that the drums carried out God's word. "Let all things be done decently and in order" 1 Corinthians 14:4, KJV.

It appears that this drummer chose to march around the steppingstones of race or skin color. This battlefield drummer was a soldier who fought to defend the "Life, Liberty, and the pursuit of Happiness" for every man, woman, and child that God had created in His image. Remember the scripture Genesis 1:27 KJV "So God created man in his own image." Once again please note. "His own image" does not mention race or skin color.

That Native Black American was born in Burlington County, New Jersey during 1752 and died in Burlington City in1853. It was reported that he was a Black man. Official records list him as mixed race. Should mixed blood hereditary be ignored? We think not! He was a true Native Black American.

Based on conclusions drawn from the evidence previously stated. It is sensible to reason that God intentionally formed Native Black Americans from the United States of America dust or soil. By His will, we are indigenous or native to and anchored in the United States of America. We are not anchored in the respected Continent of Africa.

The anchor at the beginning of High Street reminds us of wisdom in Hebrews 6:19 that has words to this effect. Our faith and hope are the anchors of the soul.

1 Thessalonians 5:22 KJV counsels us to "abstain from all appearance of evil." Perhaps in this situation the evil is…to accept the misleading racial class, African American. African American is anchored to no land mass.

With forceful determination, anchor your well-earned place in history. Accept or at the minimum, support this new racial classification "Native Black American."

Looking deeper into the mist of hidden history we can find this. Serving as land and sea armed warriors, laborers, scouts, and spies. Black Americans have distinguished themselves serving in every United States of America war.

Native Black Americans as soldiers and sailors fought for and died to help wrestle the freedom of the United States from Great Britan. Regrettably, Black Americans were denied freedom in their own Country.

It is a bitter pill to swallow, but God allowed Black Americans to suffer the brutalities of slavery, racial terrorism and being exposed to imbalanced or prejudicial treatment.

That suffering continued long after slavery officially ended.

We can suppose that inquiring minds question "My God, my God, why hast thou forsaken me?" Matthew 27:46 KJV, sends this message, God never abandoned us!

We must accept the mysteries of God; the sun rises on the evil and on the good. Matthew 5:45 KJV.

President Lincoln successfully led an initiative resulting in the passing of legislation leading to the Homestead Act. This benefit provided 160-acre plots of public land to potential homesteaders after they paid for legal paperwork. The opportunity was intended to empower potential landowners and show control of new Western territory gained by the USA Government.

While it was not a strict rule, the Homestead Act would be applicable to any civilian or soldier who had never taken up arms against the United States Government or given assistance to its enemies. Remember an examination given in Joshua 5:13 KJV. "Art thou for us, or for our adversaries?"

Other qualifications include those who were of the age 21 or greater; the head of a family; and one who is a holder of American citizenship or has filed application for citizenship in accordance with the naturalization laws.

One would have to look westward of the Mississippi River to find a large share of the new land available for Homesteading.

We are not able to identify clear-cut information revealing the numbers of Black/Colored soldiers who applied for the benefits associated with the Homestead Act opportunity. Inquiring minds likely weighed this question. Was some policy used to discourage ownership by qualified Black people.

Moving right along. Under normal conditions soldiers being discharged from service were given a sum of severance pay. They were also allowed to keep their rifles and ammunition. It was common for people to support themselves and family by hunting wild animals. From that point of view, having a rifle would certainly help with going back into civilian life.

But…There were great concerns about the impact of discharging from active duty, large numbers of Black men who had proven to be skilled warfighters. It may not be a good idea to return trained and armed men to an environment where some people would deal with them as lower-class citizens. Others would take it a step further. They would suggest that Veterans are not entitled to citizenship…because they are African Americans.

Added concerns were, although the soldiers had served under strict military regimentation, they had also experienced the privileges of being free men. The Black soldiers especially those who had over a period earned leadership power. More likely than not, would never again submit to a social order based on race driven passive behavior and agreeing to serving as a free labor source.

President Abraham Lincoln, The War Department, the Senate, and House of Representatives came up with what they reasoned to be a solution.

The Government of the United States had established the Bureau of Colored Troops to manage Black soldiers. Recruitment was slow until people such as Frederick Douglass, Harriet Tubman and other Black leaders encouraged many Black men to join the U.S. Army.

Following the end of the Civil War the possibility of Black soldiers continuing service in the Union Army presented a unique opportunity. Volunteers were recruited from the ranks of serving Black soldiers. Civilian Black men were also recruited. Buffalo Soldiers accomplished mission assignments that would contribute to setting the United States apart as a noble world power.

Black American soldiers spilled their blood fighting for the United States exhibiting a most valuable loyalty. Nevertheless, contributions by Black soldiers on the battlefield are often left out of historical records. Some history writers are driven by a desire to project supremacy, at any cost.

To the surprise of people who consider separate but equal…as equal… know this. The so-called equal treatment while serving in uniform, even today…can be a challenge. Black volunteers still answer the call to duty helping to preserve the United States as a noble world power.

The U.S Government approved the activation of new military units. The majority race filling the ranks would be Black soldiers who served in the Civil War. The new units were the 24th and 25th Infantry plus the 9th and 10th Cavalry.

The mission for the new units would include protecting the expanding railroad network and wagon trains made up of covered wagons pulled by horse/oxen animals. Another mission was to provide security for all homesteaders settling in or traveling through the new Western Territories.

There were many important benefits in deploying the newly organized Black military units. One of influential value was the meaningful and visible showing of the United States of America flag. It symbolized the power and authority of the United States of America all over its expanding territory.

Another benefit, perhaps an unintended outcome, was this proven fact. The successful security always provided by the Black soldiers made them priceless to expanding Western Railroad networks. The owners of the railroads held Black Soldiers as heroes. History keepers can be forgetful.

Retail merchants operating throughout the Western Frontier also came to rely on the trustworthy security afforded by the Buffalo Soldiers.

Even though the initial assignment was to provide security and support during Western territories expansion. Without hesitation, Buffalo soldiers regularly and successfully engaged in combat operations. But over the years. Historical accounts telling of any Black person taking part in any combat operations in the wild West, have been essentially blacked out.

We dare say that if those not so well-known events from United States history were more widely known. That could inspire a racial awakening.

Success by the Black soldiers may have been a factor leading to this unusual nickname…"Buffalo Soldiers."

According to several reports that have been told or written. Native American Indians are credited with creating the term, "Buffalo Soldiers."

The reference was more likely than not, a reference to the color of their skin, their hair texture which presents as a loose coil, and the Black Warriors' courage when facing battlefield life or death challenges. That collection of physical appearance, survival will power and fighting skills apparently provoked the American Indians to bestow the name Buffalo Soldier.

Hum…If one is willing to pause and ponder. Could the American Indians be speaking with a forked tongue or said another way. Are American Indians speaking with their tongue in the cheek when they complain about sports teams, and other organizations when they use Indian traits or images? Without much effort when looking at the name "Buffalo Soldiers" a person could reach this opinion. The carrying out of a double standard.

Double standards. Because it seems that it was acceptable to the American Indians to assign a name that refers to the values and the inherited physical appearances of Black people. However, the same is off limits for Indian.

There may have been an intent to characterize or justify their actions as an appreciation of Black people bravery. But looking into the mist one can see an image that reveals reality. "Abstain from all appearance of evil." 1 Thessalonians 5:22 KJV.

Looking back. Those pioneering Buffalo Soldiers displayed an impressive high caliber of ethical, mental, and moral strength when facing danger, fear, and stumbling stones. Choosing not to surrender to evil intents, the Black soldiers decided to embrace the legendary name…"Buffalo Soldier."

The Buffalo Soldier units consisted of Black Enlisted and Non-Commissioned Officers. Many, but not all Commanders were White.

Moving forward. There is no need to drown in deep anger for the wrongful discrimination carried out. Native Black Americans must rise above others who hate us. Present dignified behavior, practice spiritual forgiving.

We are reminded of this counsel." But I say unto you, love your enemies, bless them that curse you, do good to them that hate you, and pray for them which despitefully use you, and persecute you." Matthew 5:44 KJV.

Luke 6:48 KJV wisdom. "Like a man which built an house, and digged deep, and laid the foundation on a rock: and when the flood arose, the stream beat vehemently upon that house, and could not shake it: for it was founded upon a rock."

We do believe that there is a rock-solid foundation for this new beginning especially the new ethnic name, Native Black American. We do believe that this blessing has a solid divine origin.

This new creation cannot be shaken and torn from its foundation unless we do not have the will to fight. Unless we overcome an "already lost" state of mind. Unless we fail to prepare ourselves spiritually and academically. Unless we stop pulling other Native Black Americans down as opposed to lifting each other up.

Just as a friendly reminder, from a Biblical point of view, the number eight (8) talks to a new beginning.

We owe a debt to our ancestors who fought the good fight. Their never-ending efforts to secure freedom were like wrestling all night until the break of day. The people who were born in Africa will tell you that Native Black people born American are a different race. Get a passport if you travel to Africa.

It is normal to respect people who have earned the status of being superior to another in terms of academic success, title or rank, skills and so on.

But…Native Black Americans wrestle with people who claim supremacy based on their race, Country of birth, and several other excuses. Remember this, we cannot overlook the power and authority provided by institutions or organizations that favor one race or one ideology over another. Unjust supremacy can be reinforced when we submit it in terror.

For 5 plus generations, Native Black Americans have wrestled to gain victory in terms of "Life, Liberty, and the pursuit of Happiness." Breaking loose from the chains of unjust or prejudicial treatment by anyone.

Perhaps one of many lingering effects from slavery. Too often we have wrestled with a tendency to express disapproval of and possibly jealousy of progress earned by other Native Black Americans.

Too often we have purposely, maybe not on purpose, placed slippery steeping stones in the path of other Native Black Americans.

Without any doubt…there will be some who shall argue with those opinions just stated.

Nevertheless, anytime one surrenders to the emotional power that encourages a feeling of happiness or satisfaction when a Native Black American fails. That same person also surrenders any right to claiming the Native Black American identity…an identity that has been set aside by the Grand architect. WE must take the initiative, not leave our fate to others!

If you do not support your own race, at least those who have earned such. You are part of the tearing down rather than building up your own legacy.

Ecclesiastes 3:3 KJV give this wisdom, " A time to kill, and a time to heal; a time to break down, and a time to build up." Hum…we leave that thought for you to think about. How does it apply to your moral compass?

Earned freedom is difficult to get but has a lasting value. Unearned freedom comes with little to no effort. Its life span generally does not last.

Now, as the sun rises in the East to usher in a new day, a new beginning. Keep in mind Isaiah 60:1 KJV. "Arise, shine; for thy light is come, and the glory of the Lord is risen upon thee."

Native Black Americans must have the courage to answer the calling to lay claim on an unblemished racial identity. Once again, let it be known that we refuse to continue marching under any other constantly changing racial identity. We refuse to forcibly accept inclusion into the identity of a foreign nation. While we respect and pay honor to the esteemed Continent of Africa, Native Black Americans reject the racial name African American.

Inquiring minds may ask why. Well…there is no united agreement by American born Black people to accept integration into the identity of any existing race. However, as said many times previously, I Am who I Am. Native Black Americans not…African Americans. Let us march forward!

So…Native Black Americans. How long, how long shall some people pretend that there is some satisfaction in trying to integrate into or kidnap the racial identity of another race? How long will some accept this blemished race name, African American, a name that has multiple meaning.

How long before Native Black Americans cross over and find racial solidarity? How long before we find a sense of pride in a racial identity of our own choosing?

We must call on our faith and move forward. Remember this scripture quoted some sixteen times in the bible. "Here am I; send me"

Of those sixteen we chose this scripture…Isaiah 6:8 KJV. "Also, I heard the voice of the Lord, saying, whom shall I send, and who will go for us? Then said I, here am I; send me."

As mentioned earlier. There is no hesitation by Africans or their children to identify racially with a specific African Country. On the other hand, they generally do not identify from a nationality standpoint as Native Americans.

Native Black Americans have proven to be survivors demonstrating impressive physical and mental powers. We cannot surrender. We must be able to withstand and recover from difficult conditions with a new strength.

We must be aggressive. As stated previously, refuse limited crumbs from the King's table. Pick up your plate and turn it over, no…wait a minute. Grasp control of the empty plate presented to you and break it into pieces.

Moving forward, we need to point to very important human beings who are too often left standing in the shadows of history.

We refer to strong willed Native Black American women.

Native Black American women who repeatedly showed no signs of weakness when they voluntarily joined in defending the independence of the United States. They also helped shape the social, economic, and political structures of what was a new beginning. The United States of America as it stepped forward to earn its respected place in world history.

To make a point we decided to set aside 3 of those Native Black American women. We choose 3 because that number refers to the state of being complete. But it does not end with these 3. Revelation 1:4 KJV makes this point…"which is, and which was, and which is to come"

We are reminded of a determined Native Black American woman who was known as Harriet Tubman.

A quote attributed to Harriet Tubman. "There was one of two things I had a right to: liberty or death. If I could not have one, I would take the other, for no man should take me alive. I should fight for liberty as long as my strength lasted."

Another Harriet Tubman quote, "Twant me, 'twas the Lord. I always told him, 'I trust to you. I don't know where to go or what to do, but I expect you to lead me,' and He always did."

Could Harriet Tubman have been exposed to the biblical 15 Palms of Degrees particularly Psalm 121: 8 KJV "The Lord shall preserve thy going out and thy coming in from this time forth, and even for evermore."

If you will, pause for a second and think deeply in silence. Maybe you can suppose that Harriet Tubman lifted her eyes towards the heavens and remembered how God always kept all His promises. He never fails.

We believe that she prayed to God and leaned on her faith in Him to guide her steps. Think of Harriet asking God to bless her personal ambition to help Black people escape the evil institution called slavery.

It is a challenge to resist thinking of satisfying your own intense desires. However, Harriet Tubman realized that she needed to focus on serving the will of God and His glorification as a priority. Slavery gave many hardships.

Inquiring minds may ask, what events may lead a free person to surrender and bow down to slavery? Let us begin with the power of National, State and Municipal laws supported by implied supremacy. Beating the human body into shreds with rods and whips, known as the cat o' nine tails. Looking into a gun barrel. Legal killing (lynching). Those are just some of the very effective strategies that give reason to obey the slave masters.

Once again, clever divide and conquer schemes were effectively used to encourage servants to be obedient to them that are their masters.

Those divide and conquer tactics included but, were not limited to the forced separation of families by selling individual members to distant plantations. That truly reduced family stability and racial unity.

That scheme had a built-in plan to break up the model linking a father and mother team to lead a family. We ask…was it possible that the effects of that kind of separation would affect future generations? Today it seems to linger as a thorn in the flesh for too many Native Black American family units. We call on your viewpoint for an answer.

In the event one may ask, who was Harriet Tubman? In March 1822 she was born in The United States of America specifically the Eastern Shore area of Dorchester, Maryland. That makes her a Native Black American.

Mrs. Tubman's cradle name was Araminta which was given by her parents who were slaves.

With the passing of time, she married a man named John Tubman. She assumed the first name of her mother which was Harriet, and adopted her husband's last name.

Mrs. Tubman escaped slavery by way of Philadelphia Pa. She was an anti-slavery activist and abolitionist advocate. Driven by those beliefs, Mrs. Tubman was the principal conductor for a movement known as the Underground Railroad. A group that escorted countless slaves to freedom.

The title "Underground Railroad" as a stand-alone, can cause one to see a misleading vision.

We are not talking about the traditional railroad network. The term "Underground Railroad" is used to describe a movement organized to work secretly against the institution of slavery.

Close your eyes and imagine Harriet Tubman leading human beings as they escaped from a life of forced, unpaid labor. People labeled as slaves used many methods of messaging to include spiritual songs that contained disguised instructions. They would gather at a secret starting point which had the code name "railway station."

Led by Harriet Tubman, the escaping groups began their journeys towards the light of freedom during the hours of darkness. They walked through the forests, through swamps, over mountain ranges, in all types of weather conditions. They just seemed to slip silently from the grip of slave owners.

Another strong willed Native Black American woman was an accomplished political scientist. She has served with success as a United States of America diplomat and Presidential cabinet member.

She had the distinction of serving as the 19th and the first Native Black American Woman National Security Advisor. She was a valued advisor to the President of the United States of America from 2001 to 2005.

Because she met or exceeded numerous academic qualification standards. Because she could speak several foreign languages. Because she demonstrated impressive skills involving political matters that helped carry out national agendas. This Native Black American woman earned the privilege of becoming the first Native Black American woman to serve as the (66th) United States of America Secretary of State.

The 25th Amendment to the United States Constitution make clear the order in which or the conditions under which one person follows another to hold to a title. With that said, there is a legal process which is referred to as the Presidential succession. For the purposes of this discussion, we are basically talking to the title of the President of the United States of America.

Whenever the sitting president dies, resigns, or is removed from office. The vice president becomes acting president until another president is selected in accordance with the United States Constitution.

If the office of the vice president is unoccupied, or if the vice president is also incapacitated, presidential powers and duties are transferred in the following order. The speaker of the House of Representatives, the president pro tempore of the Senate, and then Cabinet secretaries.

The current line of Presidential succession as in pertains to Cabinet secretaries begins with the Secretary of State. Therefore, while holding the title of Secretary of State. That person, a Native Black American woman, could have briefly become the President of the United States.

Hear ye, hear ye, the United States Supreme Court is called to order.

Watch this. The first Native Black American woman was confirmed by the Senate and the House of Representatives to serve as an Associate Justice member of the United States Supreme Court.

She was nominated to the Supreme Court by President Joe Biden and sworn into office on 30 June 2022.

Sir Winston Churchill was Prime Minister of the United Kingdom from 1940 to 1945, during the Second World War, and again from 1951 to 1955. He held this viewpoint.

"Those who fail to learn from history are doomed to repeat it." One could sense similarities to words reflected in a 1905 quote by George Santayana, "Those who cannot remember the past are condemned to repeat it."

Job 12:12 KJV. "With the ancient is wisdom; and in length of days understanding." We paused for a moment of reflection. Sir Winston Churchill's and George Santayana's viewpoints could provide a beneficial model for Native Black Americans today.

We are reminded of the North American Civil War, which was fought between 1861 and 1865. It was widely referred to as the War between the States. However, that war was assigned several other names by several different groups of people for several different reasons.

Just to provide a few of those names hear this: the War of Secession, the War for Southern Independence, and the Slaveholders' Rebellion.

There were many people who counted it proper to engage in rebellion against the United States of America by declaring what in their eyes were legitimate reasons or excuses.

One much debated reason for pulling the trigger was…States Rights.

For many who were in favor of States' rights, when it is put into clear-cut language, the objective was…to defend an accepted way of doing business. A business model that stood on racially centric social-economic pillars powered by something called self-anointed supremacy.

Upholding that business model required the support of and protection of an economy that relied on unpaid labor…said another way, slavery.

Some who benefited from slavery or unpaid labor argued that each State of the Union was basically self-governing. However, under provisions contained in the U.S. Constitution, each State's sovereignty has limitations.

Looking at the entire world, slavery has left footprints throughout the history of all organized societies. Servitude, serfdom, bondage, peonage, choose your preferred title. Most religious books mention some manner of slavery.

Union states included California, Connecticut, Delaware, Illinois, Indiana, Iowa, Kentucky, Maine, Maryland, Massachusetts, Michigan, Minnesota, Missouri, New Hampshire, New Jersey, New York, Ohio, Oregon, Pennsylvania, Rhode Island, Vermont, Wisconsin, Kansas, Nevada, and West Virginia.

There were seven original secessionist southern states that formed the Confederate States of America. They included South Carolina, Mississippi, Florida, Alabama, Georgia, Louisiana, and Texas.

After the sun appeared in the Eastern sky and disappeared in the Western sky, the number of states joining the Confederacy movement increased. Involved were the States, Virginia, Arkansas, Tennessee, and North Carolina, Missouri, and Kentucky.

Of interest, diplomatic recognition of the Confederate States was never granted by Unites States of America or any foreign government.

While serving as the 16th president from 1861 to 1865. President Lincoln apparently reasoned that slavery of Black people was harmful to the United States of America and morally wrong. President Lincoln took corrective action.

If you will, hear this history which was stated in the beginning of this writing. The Emancipation Proclamation was issued on two separate occasions.

The first was published on Monday, September 22, 1862. It could be described as "a shot over the bow." The bow is the front part of a ship.

A shot over the bow is a Navy tradition that talks to firing a cannon ball across the bow of an opponent's ship to show them that you mean business! In layman's terms a warning has been properly delivered that unless a favorable proposal is received, more likely than not a battle will follow.

The first Proclamation warned the Confederate States that if those entities as identified, did not cease their rebellion by January 1st, 1863. Terms contained in the draft Emancipation Proclamation would then be put into effect.

When there was no favorable response to the first Proclamation…the following second Proclamation was issued and became immediately effective.

A transcript of words by the President of the United States of America

The Emancipation Proclamation

January 1, 1863

Whereas, on the twenty-second day of September, in the year of our Lord one thousand eight hundred and sixty-two, a proclamation was issued by the President of the United States, containing, among other things, the following, to wit:

"That on the first day of January, in the year of our Lord one thousand eight hundred and sixty-three, all persons held as slaves within any State or designated part of a State, the people whereof shall then be in rebellion against the United States, shall be then, thenceforward, and forever free; and the Executive Government of the United States, including the military and naval authority thereof, will recognize and maintain the freedom of such persons, and will do no act or acts to repress such persons, or any of them, in any efforts they may make for their actual freedom.

"That the Executive will, on the first day of January aforesaid, by proclamation, designate the States and parts of States, if any, in which the people thereof, respectively, shall then be in rebellion against the United States; and the fact that any State, or the people thereof, shall on that day be, in good faith, represented in the Congress of the United States by members chosen thereto at elections wherein a majority of the qualified voters of such State shall have participated, shall, in the absence of strong countervailing testimony, be deemed conclusive evidence that such State, and the people thereof, are not then in rebellion against the United States."

Now, therefore I, Abraham Lincoln, President of the United States, by virtue of the power in me vested as Commander-in-Chief, of the Army and Navy of the United States in time of actual armed rebellion against the authority and government of the United States, and as a fit and necessary war measure for suppressing said rebellion, do, on this first day of January, in the year of our Lord one thousand eight hundred and sixty-three, and in accordance with my purpose so to do publicly proclaimed for the full period of one hundred days, from the day first above mentioned, order and designate as the States and parts of States wherein the people thereof respectively, are this day in rebellion against the United States, the following, to wit:

Arkansas, Texas, Louisiana, (except the Parishes of St. Bernard, Plaquemines, Jefferson, St. John, St. Charles, St. James Ascension, Assumption, Terrebonne, Lafourche, St. Mary, St. Martin, and Orleans, including the City of New Orleans) Mississippi, Alabama, Florida, Georgia, South Carolina, North Carolina, and Virginia, (except the forty-eight counties designated as West Virginia, and also the counties of Berkley, Accomac, Northampton, Elizabeth City, York, Princess Ann, and Norfolk, including the cities of Norfolk and Portsmouth[)], and which excepted parts, are for the present, left precisely as if this proclamation were not issued.

And by virtue of the power, and for the purpose aforesaid, I do order and declare that all persons held as slaves within said designated States, and parts of States, are, and henceforward shall be free; and that the Executive government of the United States, including the military and naval authorities thereof, will recognize and maintain the freedom of said persons.

And I hereby enjoin upon the people so declared to be free to abstain from all violence, unless in necessary self-defence; and I recommend to them that, in all cases when allowed, they labor faithfully for reasonable wages.

And I further declare and make known, that such persons of suitable condition, will be received into the armed service of the United States to garrison forts, positions, stations, and other places, and to man vessels of all sorts in said service.

And upon this act, sincerely believed to be an act of justice, warranted by the Constitution, upon military necessity, I invoke the considerate *judgment of mankind, and the gracious favor of Almighty God.*

In witness whereof, I have hereunto set my hand and caused the seal of the United States to be affixed.

Done at the City of Washington, this first day of January, in the year of our Lord one thousand eight hundred and sixty three, and of the Independence of the United States of America the eighty-seventh.

By the President: ABRAHAM LINCOLN WILLIAM H. SEWARD, Secretary of State.

>>>>>>>>>>>>>>>>>>>>>>>>>><<<<<<<<<<<<<<<<<<<<<<<<<

We pause for a moment to reflect on a saying that is often wrongly understood or misquoted. That is "Money is the root of all evil." By intent or on purpose a key word is missing. One missing word effectively twists the intended meaning of Gods' wisdom.

1 Timothy 6:10 KJV tells us this. "For the **love** of money is the root of all evil: which while some coveted after, they have erred from the faith, and pierced themselves through with many sorrows." The key word is **love**.

It is apparent that some **loved** money more than being obedient to one of many commandments given by God.

People or businesses driven by a love of money. Loaded African men, women, and children who had been captured or purchased, into the cargo holds of sailing ships. Not as human beings but as cargo because those humans would be sold for a profit to merchants located in the South, Central, North Americas and the Caribbean territories.

Looking from the rear or aft of the ship as it sailed away. It seems easy to think of one looking back, in the direction of Africa. Surely in the mind's eye one can imagine the African countryside...slowly sinking into the Ocean.

Most ships selected for moving human cargo were sea-going class vessels. They had between 3 and 5 tall mast or poles to support giant canvas sails. Combined those mast and canvasses effectively captured the force of wind which was converted into energy. That power source forced the ship to move forward. The captured wind moving captured people. Ironic!

Knowledge captured from other sea-going people gave understanding of the Ocean movements, waves, tides, and ancient direction-finding methods.

Stay focused on the word "captured." One can assume that the captured humans who were locked up on the ships, felt abandoned. While the similarities of their worship experience with God compared to our way of worshiping Him could be a matter for debate. There is no uncertainty in this fact. Hebrews 13:5 KJV reminds us "for he hath said, I will never leave thee, nor forsake thee." Surely, He was in their mist not leaving them alone.

As Native Black Americans continue to reject surrendering to those who claim racial superiority. As we endure the thorn of prejudice in our flesh, as we keep our faith in God, we are reminded that He will always give us what we need not always what we want. Philippians 4:19 gives wisdom to this effect. "God shall supply all your needs according to His riches in glory."

We believe that one should stand still and consider the wonders of God. He has demonstrated a tendency to select certain people and set them aside to advance His kingdom. Psalm 30:5 KJV. "Weeping may endure for a night, but joy cometh in the morning." In the darkest hour, His name should be praised and glorified.

We believe that it is possible that God's plan included setting aside Africans that would cross over to become Native Black Americans...to help advance his kingdom and his word.

Diversity, Equity, and Inclusion (DEI). No Diversity was a priority when placing people from the same Tribe on the same plantation. No Equity of payment for labor. No Inclusion into benefits associated with liberty, and the pursuit of happiness. No DEI rules applied to the slave population.

Once again, we are reminded that when using the Bible as a reference, the number eight (8) talks to a new creation or new beginning.

Once again, there is no disagreement that Black Americans have a connection through some inherited appearances and other influences traceable to the Continent of Africa.

However, to all who might read this writing…let it be known that joy has come this morning. As the sun has risen and set on 5 plus generations, the point in time has finally arrived. Native Black Americans have crossed over.

Once again, the location where dust was gathered to create Native Black American men, women and children was not on the esteemed Continent of Africa. The gathering location was from the dust or soil located someplace on the territory of the prestigious United States of America.

Also changed…is our spoken and written languages and religious ways of life. Our attire, many of our dietary rules and social behaviors. For a large percentage, our genetics have changed. The result…a new creation or new beginning. Think of the principles associated with the biblical number…8.

We do give respect to and honor those who embrace the name, African American.

As for Native Black Americans. We will not agree with attempts to deny us of American citizenship. Who gave anybody the authority to integrate Native Black Americans into the nationality of Africa, a Foreign Country.

Once again, we believe that this new race, Native Black American is a part of God's plan.

Once again. We remind readers of this writing that divine intervention has resulted in the integrating of blood, inherited features, and many habits of Native Black Americans Black people with many races. A change that even includes our religious ideals. This has resulted in a recreated genetic makeup for more than a few. The outcome...a new RACE. One that is without blemish. One that is home-grown. One that is native to or indigenous to the United States of America.

Acts 17:26, KJV tells us "And hath made of one blood all nations of men for to dwell on all the face of the earth, and hath determined the times before appointed, and the bounds of their habitation."

Perhaps it was necessary as part of God's plan to allow the capture and buying of African people. And...against their will standing...in line while connected to each other by a chain around the neck. Waiting to be loaded onto cargo ships and transported to be sold in slave markets. The mass chaining of people intended to be negative had an untended positive result. Native Black Americans stand-alone forever linked together.

Perhaps it was necessary as part of God's plan that Black people were set aside to suffer for 5 plus generations. Perhaps to sharpen the steel in His plan. Proverbs 27:17 KJV "Iron sharpened iron." Romans 8:28 KJV. "And we know that all things work together for good to them that love God, to them who are the called according to his purpose."

Galatians 5:1 KJV tells us "Stand fast therefore in the liberty wherewith Christ hath made us free and be not entangled again with the yoke of bondage."

Let us pause for a monument to reflect on the Thirteenth Amendment to the Constitution governing the United States of America.

President Lincoln led an effort that resulted in the13th Amendment to the U.S. Constitution. Dated in the year 1865, that amendment was a national law that abolished slavery in the United States of America.

A transcript of the Thirteenth Amendment (XIII)

Section 1. "Neither slavery nor involuntary servitude, except as a punishment for crime whereof the party shall have been duly convicted, shall exist within the United States, or any place subject to their jurisdiction."

Section 2. "Congress shall have power to enforce this article by appropriate legislation."

Once again, President Lincoln demonstrated impressive courage. He was driven by a special ability to correctly predict and prevent what could take place in the future.

President Lincoln believed that action to influence a national law was needed to permanently free the Black slaves. An amendment to the Constitution of the United States was the only way to officially end slavery. The Proclamation Emancipation was a Presidential Executive Order (number 95).

Watch this. Persons elected to the office of President or Congress can amend or overturn an Executive order. Courts of law can declare an Executive order illegal or unconstitutional.

President Lincoln argued that the founding fathers' phrase "All men are created equal" applied to Black and White people. That should not be taken to mean that he believed Black people should share many of the rights as afforded to people who shared the race of the founding fathers.

On 18 September 1858, at Charleston, Illinois, during a political debate…Lincoln reportedly said.

"I am not, nor ever have been, in favor of bringing about in any way the social and political equality of the white and black races, that I am not, nor ever have been, in favor of making voters or jurors of negroes, nor of qualifying them to hold office, nor to intermarry with white people.

And I will say in addition that there is a physical difference between the white and black races which I believe will forever forbid the two races living together on terms of social and political equality…I will add that I have never seen, to my knowledge, a man, woman, or child who was in favor of producing a perfect equality, social and political, between negroes and white men."

Is it possible that a whisper in the ear of President Lincoln reminded him of instructions from God. "And be not conformed to this world: but be ye transformed by the renewing of your mind, that ye may prove what is that good, and acceptable, and perfect, will of God." Romans 12:2 KJV.

Psalm 84:10 KJV. "I had rather be a doorkeeper in the house of my God, than to dwell in the tents of wickedness."

Despite his language during the Charleston, Illinois debate. The words presented by President Lincoln during a speech titled the Gettysburg Address revealed changed opinions. This was a trying time.

The honesty and strength projected by President Lincoln during his speech clearly indicated a change. The moral compass of this Nation and the President pivoted. God will show us the way, if we will listen to his words.

A transcript of The Gettysburg Address
Gettysburg, Pennsylvania November 19, 1863

Four score and seven years ago our fathers brought forth on this continent, a new nation, conceived in Liberty, and dedicated to the proposition that all men are created equal.

Now we are engaged in a great civil war, testing whether that nation, or any nation so conceived and so dedicated, can long endure. We are met on a great battle-field of that war. We have come to dedicate a portion of that field, as a final resting place for those who here gave their lives that that nation might live. It is altogether fitting and proper that we should do this.

But, in a larger sense, we can not dedicate—we can not consecrate—we can not hallow—this ground.

The brave men, living and dead, who struggled here, have consecrated it, far above our poor power to add or detract. The world will little note, nor long remember what we say here, but it can never forget what they did here. It is for us the living, rather, to be dedicated here to the unfinished work which they who fought here have thus far so nobly advanced. It is rather for us to be here dedicated to the great task remaining before us—that from these honored dead we take increased devotion to that cause for which they gave the last full measure of devotion—that we here highly resolve that these dead shall not have died in vain—that this nation, under God, shall have a new birth of freedom—and that government of the people, by the people, for the people, shall not perish from the earth.

*President of the United States of America
Abraham Lincoln*

Often, the thirst for revenge can be overpowering. Sometimes we allow logic to be overruled.

In the Old Testament we find that Exodus 21:23-25 KJV, gives this guidance having to do with revenge.

Verse 23. "And if any mischief follow, then thou shalt give life for life."

Verse 24. "Eye for eye, tooth for tooth, hand for hand, foot for foot."

Verse 25. "Burning for burning, wound for wound, stripe for stripe."

In the New Testament we find that Romans 12:17-19 KJV, gives this guidance to this effect.

Verse 17. "Recompense to no man evil for evil."

Versre18. "If it be possible, as much as lieth in you, live peaceably with all men."

Verse 19. "Dearly beloved, avenge not yourselves, but rather give place unto wrath: for it is written, Vengeance is mine; I will repay, saith the Lord."

It may seem that some scriptures contradict another. To those inquiring minds who believe they see opposing guidance. Have you considered this? To understand the Holy word, one must study and pray for understanding.

John 1:1 KJV "In the beginning was the Word, and the Word was with God, and the Word was God." We believe that the original holy scriptures were inspired by God and He never contradicts Himself.

Furthermore, please keep this in mind. The exact time invested by many different people who assembled the original words of God's into several versions of the Bible or other manuscripts is uncertain. Some scholars estimate the time at 1500 years…give or take.

2 Peter 1:21KJV gives us these words. "For the prophecy came not in old time by the will of man: but holy men of God spake as they were moved by the Holy Ghost."

2 Timothy 3:16 KJV gives us these words. "All scripture is given by inspiration of God, and is profitable for doctrine, for reproof, for correction, for instruction in righteousness."

Religion is powerful, encouraging, gives hope, but it is very mysterious.

2 Peter 1:20 KJV shares this wisdom. "Knowing this first, that no prophecy of the scripture is of any private interpretation."

Could it be that the words "no prophecy of the scripture is of any private interpretation" is a way of urging people to avoid bending a scripture to support their personal Opinions? Opinions that might collide with God's will.

Proverbs 3:5 KJV reminds us that we must "Trust in the Lord with all thine heart; and lean not unto thine own understanding."

Think about this. It seems that powerful people assumed the authority to influence or control the ability to understand the intended meaning of scriptures. Their clear goal was to promote a submissive attitude by

Black people but remember Psalm 121:7 KJV. "The Lord shall preserve thee from all evil: He shall preserve thy soul."

Many Africans who had been held captives for long periods of time learned to speak the language that would boost their importance to the slave holders. In the United States…that language was English.

Several States passed anti-literacy laws which made it illegal to teach slaves to read and write English. But if the goal was to urge obedience and defeat rebellion. Teaching slaves to read Bibles seemed to collide with those anti-literacy laws.

An intense effort focused on Christian based religious studies was introduced to the slaves. However, there was a ram in the bush or a hidden benefit. The Africans used Bible studies as a tool to learn how to read and write English. God works in mysterious ways. No man will be allowed to pluck God's creation out of His hand…unless He allows such to happen.

The slave traders and plantation owners assumed that it would be easier to control the Black slaves if they could be convinced that slavery was approved by God. In other words, if the Holy Bible scriptures said slavery was right. The Black people would bow down and submit.

Abolitionists or groups of people who advocated officially ending slavery were gaining popular support and political strength. The abolitionist and other groups also urged a stronger acceptance of Christianity by the slave population. However, the objective was to encourage the worship of God.

Ironically, history points to this fact. Hundreds of years before the birth of slavery in the Americas. The same hand that wrote the10 Commandments reached out and planted seeds of the Abrahamic religions on the fertile soil of Africa. Abrahamic religions include Judaism, Christianity, and Islam. It seems that Black people did in fact have knowledge of God's moral guidelines before the Negro or Slave Bibles.

When the Africans found themselves held in captivity and classified as chattel like domestic animals. Basically, they were personal property that could be bought, traded or sold! They had reason to feel discouraged. More likely than not, considering those conditions. It could rise as a challenge to inspire any man or woman of any race to be faithful believers or followers of any religion.

Let us pause and look at the religious books titled either Slave or Negro Bibles. Scriptures were in the Bibles that could be used as a basis to justify slavery or inspire submission. However, other scriptures that might bring about an uprising or make stronger the desire for freedom were left out.

Read the following Scriptures in Negro or Slave Bibles that might have served as a basis to justify slavery or inspire submission.

1. "Ephesians 6:5 KJV. "Servants, be obedient to them that are your masters according to the flesh, with fear and trembling, in singleness of your heart, as unto Christ."

2. "Titus 2:9 KJV. "Exhort servants to be obedient unto their own masters, and to please them well in all things; not answering again."

3. "1 Peter 2:18 KJV. "Servants, be subject to your masters with all fear; not only to the good and gentle, but also to the froward."

Read the following Scriptures that were left out because they might bring about an uprising or make stronger the desire for freedom.

1. "1.Exodus 21:16 KJV. "And he that stealeth a man, and selleth him, or if he be found in his hand, he shall surely be put to death."

2. "Exodus 8:1 KJV. "And the Lord spake unto Moses, Go unto Pharaoh, and say unto him, Thus saith the Lord, Let my people go, that they may serve me."

3. "Jeremiah 22:13 KJV. "Woe unto him that buildeth his house by unrighteousness, and his chambers by wrong; that useth his neighbour's service without wages, and giveth him not for his work."

4. "Exodus 22:23-24-26 "And if any mischief follow, then thou shalt give life for life; Eye for eye, tooth for tooth, hand for hand, foot for foot; Burning for burning, wound for wound, stripe for stripe."

There have been studies which support that at an unspecified point in time. Africans began to form clicking like noises, and other mixed sounds which at the end of the day developed into syllables. Looking back many years, that process of evolution gave birth to four basic African language groups. We are pointing to the birth of logical spoken and written language groups across the Continent of Africa.

Therefore, without any doubt there is evidence that before slavery in the Americas, Africans had developed the ability to exchange information in writing and using spoken sentences. But...because they spoke and wrote in a language not understood by most people who were consumed with human trafficking. African hostages were marketed as illiterate people.

Again, teaching slaves to read and understand the English language using Slave or Negro Bibles seemed not to focus on submitting to the will of God. Instead, the effort seemed to focus on inspiring slaves to submit to the will of slave owners. It does not matter if the focus was by chance or by design hear this wisdom. Galatians 6:7 KJV. "Be not deceived; God is not mocked: for whatsoever a man soweth, that shall he also reap."

1 Corinthians 3:7 KJV can lead to this inspiration. God never fails. He can with intent plant a good seed. However, every man can pursue his own reward according to his own labor. God has ordered the steps of people who would become Native Black Americans. Now, they must prove themselves worthy.

Ponder the thoughts of the framers, writers, approving powers, and the signers of the United States Declaration of Independence, the Bill of Rights, and the United States Constitution. Maybe when thinking through the words of those documents. The view declaring that "all Men are created equal" may not have had Black slaves in mind. Just as a reminder; Genesis 1:27 KJV. "God created man in his own image, in the image of God created he male and female."

Once again, it really did not matter. We believe that in the beginning when He created man in his own image. God...had already thought through a racial makeover. The creation of Native Black Americans to serve His will.

The United States Constitution does speak to "All persons **born** or **naturalized**." Those words are powerful. Here we find one of many standards that empowers a separation of the racial classifications... Native Black Americans...from African American.

By the will of God and by the authority of the Constitution of the United States. Native Black Americans who were born on U.S.A. soil, are blessed to be United States of America citizens.

For the record. Most Native Black Americans who represent a group that could be referred to as the silent majority. Solidly reject the unwanted racial name "African American.

We previously pointed to this fact. It is not unusual for people who were blessed to be born on the Continent of Africa. Despite acquiring naturalized citizenship. As a rule, they do not hesitate to identify their own race consistent with the birth Country of their parents.

If you will, come with us to review the 14th Amendment to the U.S. Constitution.

A transcript of the Fourteenth Amendment (XIV)

Section 1. Passed by Congress June 13, 1866, and ratified July 9, 1868.

All persons born or naturalized in the United States, and subject to the jurisdiction thereof, are citizens of the United States and of the State wherein they reside. No State shall make or enforce any law which shall abridge the privileges or immunities of citizens of the United States; nor shall any State deprive any person of life, liberty, or property, without due process of law; nor deny to any person within its jurisdiction the equal protection of the laws.

Section 2

Representatives shall be apportioned among the several States according to their respective numbers, counting the whole number of persons in each State, excluding Indians not taxed. But when the right to vote at any election for the choice of electors for President and Vice-President of the United States, Representatives in Congress, the Executive and Judicial officers of a State, or the members of the Legislature thereof, is denied to any of the male inhabitants of such State, being twenty-one years of age, and citizens of the United States, or in any way abridged, except for participation in rebellion, or other crime, the basis of representation therein shall be reduced in the proportion which the number of such male citizens shall bear to the whole number of male citizens twenty-one years of age in such State.

Section 3

No person shall be a Senator or Representative in Congress, or elector of President and Vice-President, or hold any office, civil or military, under the United States, or under any State, who, having previously taken an oath, as a member of Congress, or as an officer of the United States, or as a member of any State legislature, or as an executive or judicial officer of any State, to support the Constitution of the United States, shall have engaged in insurrection or rebellion against the same, or given aid or comfort to the enemies thereof. But Congress may by a vote of two-thirds *of each House, remove such disability.*

Section 4

The validity of the public debt of the United States, authorized by law, including debts incurred for payment of pensions and bounties for services in suppressing insurrection or rebellion, shall not be questioned. But neither the United States nor any State shall assume or pay any debt or obligation incurred in aid of insurrection or rebellion against the United States, or any claim for the loss or emancipation of any slave; but all such debts, obligations and claims shall be held illegal and void.

Section 5

The Congress shall have the power to enforce, by appropriate legislation, the provisions of this article.

The 14th Amendment is exact and clear as it relates to Black people who were created from the soil of…or said another way…born in the United States of America. Effective June 13, 1866, all persons born in the United States are citizens. When any child is born to a Black slave in the United States especially after 5 plus generations…that child is a citizen. Therefore, their correct National identity is Native Black American. Not African American.

Andrew Johnson served as the 7th president of the United States of America. For several years he supported opposition to any language that could breathe life into the 14th amendment.

But watch this. The 14th Amendment became a national law. Since the Amendment breathed life into the privilege of and entitlement to citizenship for Native Black Americans. We became eligible to pursue and enjoy rewards or benefits available to the general American public. Don't overlook this truth. The difference between the words privilege and entitlement can be fuzzy.

Privilege talks about benefits that are unearned, but they are within reach. Typically, privilege is powered by however, not limited to laws and customs, social class, titles, finances, place of birth, body features and street addresses.

Entitlement talks about benefits that either you have earned, or they are set by laws or customs. Typically, entitlement is powered by however, not limited to religious or value-based groups, liberty, educational diplomas or certificates, finances, attitudes, your contributions to society, and titles.

Yes…Governments will lay down rules that could put liberty within the reach of all. However, real liberty must be powered by faith in God, brainpower, hard work, service on the battlefield, and obeying laws of the society in which you live.

It is reliable to believe this. Had not opposing visions breathed life into conditions that led to the Civil War. The Civil War would not have breathed life into the 13th Amendment of the Constitution. For the record, that Amendment abolished legal slavery in the United States.

And…if not for the 13th Amendment. Native Black Americans might not have secured the privileged to breath…as free citizens. We are reminded of Galatians 5:1 KJV. "Stand fast therefore in the liberty wherewith Christ hath made us free and be not entangled again with the yoke of bondage." God always keeps his promises. If He had not allowed events to breathe life into the 13th Amendment. Slavery in the United States may have endured forever and a day.

As stated before, we give honor to and respect those who insist on agreeing to the assignment of African American as their national identification.

Ephesians 4:14 KJV. "That we henceforth be no more children, tossed to and fro, and carried about with every wind of doctrine, by the sleight of men, and cunning craftiness, whereby they lie in wait to deceive."

Close your eyes and see visions of Native Black Americans who have survived for centuries while being tossed about like a wave in a stormy sea. People who refuse to cross over to Native Black American will condemn their descendants to be tossed to and fro and carried about with every wind of doctrine imposed by self-anointed supremist, who lie in wait to deceive.

If you will come with us. Imagine being present to hear a very passionate speech presented by Patrick Henry at the Second Virginia Convention in 1775. William Wirt is said to have reassembled Patrick Henry's speech.

Patrick Henry made a noble testimony which included words to this effect. "Why stand we here idle? What is it that gentlemen wish? What would they have? Is life so dear, or peace so sweet, as to be purchased at the price of chains and slavery? Forbid it, Almighty God! I know not what course others may take; but as for me, give me liberty or give me death!"

When it comes to accepting the racial naming, African American, a title that essentially lacks exact labeling or absolute attributes. We say no. As for Native Black Americans, we pray that God will bless us by anointing this new unblemished racial name. It is a good name. Proverbs 22:1, KJV reminds us of words to this effect. A good name is to be chosen rather than great riches.

Reference Acknowledgements

King James Version (KJV) Public Domain

Wikipedia.org

Wikipedia, the free encyclopedia

USimmigration.org/glossary/citizenship

www.history.com/news/5-things-you-may-not-know.

Indigenous definition and meaning | Collins English Dictionary

Patrick Henry oratory in 1775

The Emancipation Proclamation | National Archives

www.thefreedictionary.com

Merriam-Webster

Cambridge English Dictionary

Oxford Dictionaries

www.dictionary.com

www.yourdictionary.com/mythology

Courtesy U.S. National Archives (1667751)

www.loc.gov/.../abraham-lincoln-and-emancipation

www.archives.gov/education/lessons/blacks-civil-war

www.brainyquote.com/quotes/harry_s_truman_398848

www.va.gov/opa/publications/celebrate/pledge

www.biblestudy.org/bibleref/meaning-of-numbers

lisbdnet.com/why-does-the-earth-orbit-the-sun

www.biblestudy.org/bibleref/meaning-of-numbers

www.britannica.com/